PREPARED TO GIVE AN ANSWER

PREPARED TO GIVE AN ANSWER

Peter Thomas

books.pbthomas.com

http://www.fast-print.net/bookshop

PREPARED TO GIVE AN ANSWER

A catalogue record for this book is available from the British Library

ISBN 978-178456-379-0

First Published 2016 by
Fast-Print Publishing of Peterborough, England.

For my wonderful wife Ruth
and our amazing family Lizzie, Susie and David.
With gratitude to Nick and Linda for their tireless encouragement and inspiration.
And for the members and friends of North Springfield Baptist Church who live what it means to be the church

Contents

Introduction

"I wish I could have more conversations about Jesus." Christians long to talk about Jesus Christ and share their faith with their friends and neighbours and colleagues. But many are scared that they won't know what to say. We are afraid we will say the wrong things, or that people will ask us questions we cannot answer. The aim of this book is to help Christians to be more confident and wise, bold and effective in talking about Jesus.

Part 1, Questions People Ask, suggests the kinds of answers Christians might give to the most common questions on spiritual topics. Each chapter presents lines of thinking, Bible verses, memorable quotations and simple illustrations which will help Christians develop their own answers to the questions. We will be less afraid of talking about Jesus when we have in our minds some answers we might offer.

Part 2, Talking About Jesus, considers practically the general subject of why and how Christians can share our faith. We need to be taking steps to equip ourselves to take every opportunity to talk about Jesus: *always be prepared to give an answer.* (1 Peter 3:15). Starting by praying, we need to overcome the barriers which make us anxious about talking about our faith and about spiritual topics. We can prepare ourselves to share our experiences of the difference Jesus makes to our lives. And by reflecting on Part 1 we can think through the kinds of answers we can give to the questions people are really asking about faith and spirituality.

My hope and prayer is that this book will give practical help and encouragement so that Christians will indeed be *prepared to give an answer* – so that we can all talk more about Jesus.

Peter Thomas

North Springfield Baptist Church – June 2016

PART 1

QUESTIONS PEOPLE ASK

1 What is salvation?

Soon after the first Easter, the apostle Peter was explaining the Good News about Jesus. His vital message was this. *"It is by the name of Jesus Christ of Nazareth, whom you crucified but whom God raised from the dead, that this man stands before you healed. Salvation is found in no one else, for there is no other name under heaven given to men by which we must be saved." (Acts 4:10,12)*
God gives His gift of salvation through the historic events of the death and resurrection of Jesus Christ. We can only be saved through Jesus.

The Bible talks a lot about salvation. We find that word in 127 places and the idea of being saved more than 300 times in the Bible. Jesus talked a lot about salvation. And the church talks a lot about salvation, because "being saved" is at the heart of the Christian faith. But what is salvation? What does it mean to be "saved"?

Salvation is an umbrella word for all wonderful blessings God gives to His people. In the Old Testament it meant rescue from slavery in Egypt in the Exodus, deliverance from evil and redemption from captivity. In the New Testament salvation embraces forgiveness of sins, escape from judgment and God's free gift of life in all its fullness, eternal life which not even death can take away. Through the ages the church has been described as "the ark of salvation" and we find a very helpful picture of salvation in the idea of being rescued in a lifeboat.

The historical dockyards at Chatham host a fascinating exhibition of lifeboats provided by the Royal National Lifeboat Institution from early simple sailing boats to recent lifeboats. Each boat on display has a sign showing how many times it had been launched and how many lives it had saved. Over the years many thousands of lives have been saved by lifeboats. From the safety of the shore I once watched a rescue taking place in a storm. Ever since I have been especially grateful that I have never had to be rescued at sea. If you are on a ship which is sinking I can imagine what a wonderful relief it must be to see a lifeboat arrive and to climb aboard! Maybe you are already in the icy water, being battered by the wind and the waves, struggling to stay afloat. You need to be saved. How wonderful to see a lifeboat! You are pulled on board – you have been saved from the sea which was about to swallow you up. As you get out of wet clothes into a dry blanket and sip warm tea you are being saved. And when you arrive on dry land you will finally be completely safe. You have been saved, you are being saved and you will be saved. This gives us a picture of what salvation means to Christians.

We have been saved. Not from the sea and the wind and the waves but from something even more deadly – one hundred percent fatal. Saved from ourselves. Rescued from our own selfishness and self-centredness. Saved from pride and greed and self-sufficiency which drag us down to our doom just as much as any stormy sea. Rescued from all the bad things we do and say and think which the Bible calls sin which separate us from the God who made us and loves us.

Only Jesus can save us. That is what Easter is all about. They call it "Good" Friday because on that day Jesus Christ the Son of God laid down his life for us, so that we could be forgiven. *Christ had no sin, but God made him to be sin for us so that in Him we could become the righteousness of God.* (2 Corinthians 5:21) Then on Easter Day God raised Jesus to life again. Jesus is alive! So when we put our trust in Jesus our sins are forgiven and through God's gift we also share in Jesus's resurrection life.

We have been saved, and we are being saved. Just as a person rescued from drowning sitting on the lifeboat headed for shore enjoys simple blessings of being alive, warm clothes, food and a warm drink, so Christians enjoy God's rich blessings here and now: God's presence, peace and joy; the privilege of prayer; the friendship and community of the church and God living inside us as the Holy Spirit. Jesus called all these things "life in all its fullness." *"I have come that they might have life, and have it more abundantly,"* Jesus said (John 10:10). Christians experience "eternal life", a personal relationship with God and Jesus which not even death can take away.

We have been saved, we are being saved, and the Bible also says we will be saved. The lifeboat has yet to reach the shore. When it does, the best is yet to come. Because being saved is not just for this life, but forever. When this earthly life is over, we have the happy certainty of being with God forever. We aren't afraid of dying – our life will continue in heaven.

We have been saved, we are being saved and we will be saved. That is what Christians understand by salvation. That is why we are so happy to be saved.

I remember a poster of a beautiful butterfly with a Bible verse on it. It read,
When a person becomes a Christian he becomes a brand new person inside.
He is not the same any more. A new life has begun! (2 Corinthians 5:17)

Just as a caterpillar changes into a butterfly, in the same way when a person is saved a whole new life begins. John Newton was a slave trader, but God reached into his life and transformed him and he wrote the inspiring hymn Amazing Grace.
"Amazing grace – how sweet the sound, that saved a wretch like me!
I once was lost, but now I'm found. Was blind, but now I see."

The starting point, of course, is for a person to realise they need saving. We all need saving. This world is a sinking ship and every one of us is adrift on the ocean and doomed to ending up sinking to the depths. Every one of us have things in our lives which we have done or said which we are ashamed of. We all need saving. It is said that Sir Arthur Conan Doyle, creator of Sherlock Holmes, one played a joke on a dozen influential people, businessmen, politicians, even clergymen. He sent them all identical telegrams, "Flee at once all is discovered!" The story goes that within 24 hours all of them had left the country. We all need rescuing from ourselves.

As a teenager I did not think I needed saving. I didn't grow up in a Christian family. We never went to church or Sunday school or talked about God. By the time I was studying science in the sixth form I was convinced that science had proved that God didn't exist. Then some school friends invited me along to their church youth club. I started going along to their Bible Studies as well to show them that their ideas about Jesus were all wrong. I won all the arguments, but they never got angry with me. And then one night I realised that these friends were all nice people, kind people, friendly people, the kind of person I wished I could be, but I knew I wasn't. So for the first time in my life I prayed to the God I didn't really believe in. It was a very simple prayer: "God change me!" The next morning, I woke up and the whole world was very different. I just knew deep inside that God existed and that God loved me, even me. And somehow I knew that God had forgiven me for all the things I do wrong and all my selfishness and pride. I had begun to discover all the great things which are wrapped up in the wonderful experience of salvation. That was 40 years ago. My life is still a work in progress but I know that God has rescued me.

We all need saving. We can't save ourselves. Only Jesus can save us. We need to send out a call for help. S.O.S. – save our souls. I remember another poster with a picture of a rescue helicopter winching a sailor up from a boat sinking in a stormy sea. The caption on the poster said this. "*How shall we escape if we ignore such a great salvation?*" (Hebrews 2:3)

The story of the sinking of the Titanic teaches us a valuable lesson. As the unsinkable ship disappeared beneath the waves taking 1517 people to their deaths there were still empty seats on the lifeboats. Some people did not realise the danger they were facing. They did not know they needed to be rescued. Equally today, there are many empty seats in the Lifeboat of Salvation. There are some people swimming around in the water, realising they aren't waving but drowning, yet still they do not get into the lifeboat. Other people are still aboard their own Titanic, thinking they are completely safe, eating their dinners, listening to the band, lounging in their deckchairs sipping their drinks not recognising that the ship is sinking and that unless they get aboard the lifeboat they are doomed. The Lifeboat of Salvation has room for everybody. But each person has to choose for themselves to get aboard. A simple story makes the point: the parable of the two drowning men.

Two men fell into a river. One man could swim – the other one could not. The current was strong and was carrying them towards a dangerous waterfall. One of the men drowned, the other one was saved. Which man do you think it was who survived?

It was the man who could not swim who survived. When onlookers on the bank threw a lifebuoy to the man who could not swim, he took firm hold of it. The onlookers pulled on the rope and pulled the man who could not swim to safety on dry land.

But when the onlookers threw a lifebuoy to the man who could swim, he ignored it. He kept on swimming towards the shore but the current was too strong for him. Still he refused to take hold of the lifebuoy and he was carried over the waterfall. So the man who could swim was drowned. But the man who could not swim was saved.

"How shall we escape if we ignore such a great salvation?"

2 What is the point of life?

Jesus said, *"The kingdom of heaven is like treasure hidden in a field. When a man found it, he hid it again, and then in his joy went and sold all he had and bought that field. … the kingdom of heaven is like a merchant looking for fine pearls. When he found one of great value, he went away and sold everything he had and bought it.* (Matthew 13:44-46)

The largest pearl in the world is called the pearl of Allah. It is more than 9 inches long and weighs over 6 kg. It is valued at more than thirty million pounds. The largest cut diamond in the world is called the Golden Jubilee. It weighs 545 carats and is valued at somewhere between three million and nine million pounds. The second largest diamond used to be the Great Star of Africa which weighs 530 carats and is set in the Royal Sceptre in the Crown Jewels on display in the Tower of London. Due to its setting and history its value is estimated at over three hundred million pounds, not that Her Majesty is planning on selling it. However, a 1,111 carat diamond has recently been found in Botswana and that will be shaped into the second largest cut diamond.

Until recently the most expensive champagne you could buy was Cristal Brut 1990 and a Methuselah 6 litre bottle cost $17,625. Then 200 bottles of Heidsieck Champagne were found. They were bottled in 1907 but lost in a shipwreck in 1916 and only recovered in 1997. Those 110-year-old bottles of vintage champagne are now sold in the Ritz-Carlton hotel in Moscow for $275,000 a bottle. Yet in terms of the price per litre, champagne is only the third most expensive liquid. Arguments rage whether the most expensive readily available liquid is Chanel No 5 perfume, or that substance commonly referred to as liquid gold, ink for inkjet printers which can cost as much as £10,000 per litre.

All kinds of thing are said to be worth their weight in gold. Gold is trading at around £710 per troy ounce or £22,830 per kilogram. So an average person carrying all they could might be able to lift somewhere between half a million and a million pounds' worth of gold. And then there are some very valuable things you could buy but which you couldn't carry around with you. The most expensive house in England is a six-storey Grade 1 listed Regency mansion just a stone's throw from

Buckingham Palace. That house is valued at two hundred and fifty million pounds.

We could call these expensive items priceless if we didn't have a price for them. But surely some things in life are much more precious than objects. What is the point of life? Surely life is about more than possessions. Surely life is about more than money. Some things in life are more valuable than all the money and all the possessions you could ever have. More precious than buried treasure. More precious than any pearl of great value. More precious than diamonds or gold or great big houses or a champagne lifestyle. So many people in Britain today are materially overfed but spiritually starving. So what is the point of life?

Jesus said in John 10:10, *"I have come that they may have life, and have it to the full."* (New International Version). To *"have life and have it more abundantly."* (Revised Standard Version) That is the amazing free gift which God wants to give us all through Jesus. *"Life in all its fullness."* (Good News Bible) *"A rich and satisfying life."* (New Living Translation) *"I came so they can have real and eternal life, more and better life than they ever dreamed of."* (The Message Translation) This life in all its fullness brings us so many wonderful blessings.

Love – knowing that God loves us and that His love will never let us go.

Joy – not the passing happiness which so many people look for in false gods such as Money and Entertainment, but true joy which no-one and nothing can take away.

Peace – the inner calm of knowing that everything is safe in the loving hands of Almighty God.

Eternal life – a quality of life which not even death can take away.

Freedom – to live life in a way which is pleasing to God. *"The glorious liberty of the children of God"* (Romans 8:21). Jesus said, *"If the son shall set you free you will be free indeed."* (John 8:32)

Jesus explained what eternal life and life in all its fullness are really about in John 17:3. *"Now this is eternal life: that they may know you, the only true God, and Jesus Christ, whom you have sent."* That is what eternal life really is all about – to know God and to know Jesus. That is the real point of life: the joy of experiencing a personal relationship with God.

Three hundred years ago churches were drawing up a statement of what Christians believe and they asked this question. "What is the chief end of man?" In today's language – what are human beings created for? What is their purpose? What is their destiny? What is the point of life? And the answer they came ups with was this. "The chief end of man is to glorify God and to enjoy Him forever." Even earlier, back in the fifth century Augustine said this. "You have made us for yourself, O Lord, and our hearts are restless until they find their rest in you." This is the truth about the point of life. Human beings were created to experience a relationship with God. Without God our lives will never be complete. We will always have a 'God-shaped gap' in our lives which nothing but God can fill.

In the seventeenth century the French mathematician and Christian philosopher Blaise Pascal explained it like this.

> "What else does this craving, and this helplessness, proclaim but that there was once in man a true happiness, of which all that now remains is the empty print and trace? This he tries in vain to fill with everything around him, seeking in things that are not there the help he cannot find in those that are, though none can help, since this infinite abyss can be filled only with an infinite and immutable object; in other words by God himself."

What is the point of life? It is to glorify God and to enjoy Him forever. It is to receive that eternal life which consists of a personal relationship with the Living God: life in all its fullness. God has made it possible for human beings to know Him through Jesus Christ. Through Jesus, God has made a way to forgive our sins. There's no real point in being forgiven in and of itself. The whole point of forgiveness is that God has dealt with the sin which separated fallen human beings from the Holy God. The purpose of forgiveness is so that we can experience a relationship with God; that relationship with God for which we were designed and created. Sin has spoiled humanity's relationship with God. But now the barrier of sin has been removed we can come to know God as He knows us. Every human being can enjoy this personal relationship with God.

Some people misunderstand this point. They think that eternal life is some mysterious spiritual something, some quality of life which God gives to Christians which stays with them forever. Eternal life is not like that at all. Some Christians mistakenly expect that love and joy and peace and victory and freedom are experiences which will come to us in some way apart from God, separate from God Himself. But that is not the way it works. Love and joy and peace and victory and freedom do come to Christians, but they come through our relationship with God and not apart from Him. Knowing God brings us love and joy and peace and victory and freedom. But we only experience these blessings from and through our relationship with God.

To be absolutely clear, our relationship with God is not some means by which we can enjoy blessings like love and joy and peace and victory and freedom. Knowing God is not a means to anything. Knowing God is the most worthy and desirable and glorious end in itself. All the wonderful blessings of salvation we could name are incidental to the true blessing which is the blessing of knowing God. Eternal life consists of that relationship with God and there are no blessings which come outside of that relationship with God!

Christians believe in the God who is Father, Son and Holy Spirit, three persons in one substance, God the three in one, the Holy Trinity. God Himself, within Himself, is relationship and community. In our salvation God invites us to enter into and participate in that Divine Community. At the same time, we become part of another never-ending community, God's forever family, the body of Christ, the church. This is the key to understanding what salvation and eternal life are all about. Eternal life is experiencing this amazing relationship with the Almighty and Eternal God.

Jesus compared himself to a shepherd and called himself the Good Shepherd. *"The sheep listen to his voice. He calls his own sheep by name and leads them out. When he has brought out all his own, he goes on ahead of them, and his sheep follow him because they know his voice."* (John 10:3-4)
"My sheep listen to my voice; I know them, and they follow me. I give them eternal life, and they shall never perish; no one can snatch them out of my hand."
(John 10:27-28)

Jesus the Son of God promises His disciples that we will have the same kind of intimate relationship with God the Father as he himself enjoys. *I will ask the Father, and he will give you another Counsellor to be with you for ever – the Spirit of truth. ... you know him, for he lives with you and will be in you. I will not leave you as orphans; I will come to you. .... On that day you will realise that I am in my Father, and you are in me, and I am in you. .... My Father will love him, and we will come to him and make our home with him."* (John 14:16-18, 20, 23)

That close personal relationship with God is what Jesus prays for all his followers. "*Father, just as you are in me and I am in you. May they also be in us ... that they may be one as we are one: I in them and you in me. ... in order that the love you have for me may be in them and that I myself may be in them.*"
(John 17:21-23, 26)

This is what eternal life is – that relationship with God, God living in us, Father Son and Holy Spirit making their home in us. Christians experience our relationship with God in a variety of ways. The most important are also the most obvious – prayer, Bible Study, worship, fellowship with our Christian brothers and sisters in the church and of course communion through sharing bread and wine. These are not just ways which God might choose to bless us. They are the ways in which we talk to God and He talks to us. They are the ways by which we receive the joy and peace which come from loving God and knowing He loves us. They are the ways in which we experience that victory and that freedom which come from our relationship with God. We delight in praying and reading the Bible and worshipping God because these are the ways we experience that relationship with God which is what eternal life is all about.

So how can we experience more of this fullness of life which Jesus promises us? Some Christians expect that all they have to do is just sit around, and then love and joy and peace and victory and freedom will flood into their lives. They have missed the point. We will only enjoy those blessings as we experience and enjoy our relationship with God.

For example, think about prayer. God promises, "*the peace of God, which transcends all understanding, will guard your hearts and your minds in Christ Jesus.*" (Philippians 4:7) But the way we come to experience that wonderful peace God gives is through prayer.

Do not be anxious about anything, but in everything, by prayer and petition, with thanksgiving, present your requests to God. (Philippians 4:6)

The old hymn puts it this way.
"What a friend we have in Jesus, all our sins and griefs to bear.
What a privilege to carry everything to God in prayer.
Oh what peace we often forfeit, O what needless pain we bear.
All because we do not carry everything to God in prayer."

God's peace comes to us through our relationship with God which lets us commit every part of our lives to Him in prayer. As he writes to the Philippian church, Paul continues, … *I have learned to be content whatever the circumstances. …. I can do everything through him who gives me strength.* (Philippians 4:11,13) God gives us wonderful contentment and divine strength. But these do not come to us in abstract. They come as we enjoy communion with God and He gives us His strength.

The Old Testament prophet Isaiah says, *"You will keep him in perfect peace whose mind is fixed on you, because he trusts in you."* (Isaiah 26:3) So our peace comes from the continuing act of fixing our minds on God, relying on him and consciously putting our trust in him.

Joy is exactly the same. It comes from our relationship with God. *You have made known to me the path of life; you will fill me with joy in your presence, with eternal pleasures at your right hand.* (Psalm 16:11)

Joy comes from being in the presence of God. It makes little sense for some people to say they are eager to get to heaven to spend eternity in God's presence, if they don't delight in spending time with God now. The chief end of man, the destiny of human beings, the purpose for which we were created, is to glorify God and to enjoy Him forever. Our job on earth is to learn to enjoy God. That is what life in all its fullness is all about.

Psalm 37:3-4 says this. *Trust in the LORD and do good; dwell in the land and enjoy safe pasture. Delight yourself in the LORD and he will give you the desires of your heart.*
We receive everything we most desire and everything we most need, when we learn to delight ourselves in the Lord.

Christians delight in God and we get to know God through prayer. We should not treat prayer as merely a useful tool to help us in our Christian lives. Richard Foster wrote, "Prayer is nothing more than our ongoing and growing love relationship with God the Father, Son and Holy Spirit." Prayer is the heart of our relationship with God.

Then we also spend time with God by reading and studying our Bibles. John Stott called the Bible "God's love letter to the church." It tells us how much God loves us. We should want to spend time listening to what God has to say to us. And we spend time with God in worship – giving time to praise and thanksgiving and adoration. Worship is God's children rejoicing in God's presence. If we want to enjoy our salvation we need to devote time to meeting with God, by ourselves and with others.

In his book, The Root of the Righteous, my favourite devotional author, A.W.Tozer wrote this.

> "The Christian is strong or weak depending upon how closely he has cultivated the knowledge of God. Paul devoted his whole life to the art of knowing Christ. He wrote, *"All I want is to know Christ."* …. Progress in the Christian life is exactly equal to the growing knowledge we gain of ... God in personal experience. And such experience requires a whole life devoted to it and plenty of time spent at the holy task of cultivating God. God can be known satisfactorily only as we devote time to Him.
> "A thousand distractions would woo us away from thoughts of God, but if we are wise we will sternly put them from us and make room for the King and take time to entertain Him. Some things may be neglected with but little loss to the spiritual life, but to neglect communion with God is to hurt ourselves where we cannot afford it. God will respond to our efforts to know Him. The Bible tells us how; it is altogether a matter of how much determination we bring to the holy task."

In the Sermon on the mount, Jesus taught, *"Blessed are those who hunger and thirst for God, for they will be satisfied!"* God really wants us to know Him better, to love Him more and more, and to "enjoy Him forever". That is what eternal life is all about – this personal relationship with God our Heavenly Father.

Imagine if you will the tragedy of a marriage which has gone wrong. The husband and the wife never speak to each other and never spend time together. He does all the cooking and prepares all the meals but they never eat together. Although she always does the washing up he never says thank you. He leaves dirty clothes around which she washes and irons but never sees him wearing them. He never sees her to say thank you. That is not what marriage should be. The chores are there but the relationship is not. That is a picture of what some people mistakenly think life as a Christian should be like.

The story is told of a husband and wife who never spoke to each other anymore. They only communicated by sending one another notes. The wife always got up early and the husband rather later but one day he had a very important early meeting. So the night before he wrote his wife a note explaining the situation and asking her to be sure to wake him up the next morning at seven o'clock. When he woke up the following morning it was already nine o'clock and he had missed his meeting. The husband was so upset he actually spoke aloud to his wife. "Why on earth didn't you wake me up?" he asked. The wife just pointed to a note she had left on the husband's pillow. In loud capital letters the note read, "WAKE UP - IT'S SEVEN O'CLOCK!"

That is another sad parable of the way some Christians miss out on life in all its fullness. The blessings of eternal life are all wrapped up in a personal relationship with the living God. A.W.Tozer said "We are called to an everlasting preoccupation with God." To glorify God and enjoy Him forever. But Christians will not enjoy eternal life or experience life in all its fullness if we can't be bothered to spend time with God praying and reading our Bibles and worshipping and meeting with other Christians. Because our relationship with God is the heart of life in all its fullness. Eternal life consists of our personal relationship with God. And that is the point of life.

3 How can we have a relationship with God?

We have thought about salvation and what it means to be saved. We have discovered that the whole point of life is to have a relationship with the Living God. But how has God made such a wonderful relationship possible? A very clear answer to that question can be found by unpacking just a few crucial verses of the apostle Paul's letter to the Romans chapter 3 which lay out what it means to be saved, why we need to be saved, and just how God has saved us.

God's plan of salvation

[21] *But now a* ***righteousness*** *from God, apart from law, has been made known, to*
which the Law and the Prophets testify. [22] *This righteousness from God comes through*
faith in Jesus Christ to all who believe. There is no difference, [23] ***for all have***
sinned *and fall short of the glory of God,* [24] *and are* ***justified*** *freely by his grace*
through the ***redemption*** *that came by Christ Jesus.* [25] *God presented him as a*
sacrifice of atonement*, through faith in his blood.* (Romans 3:21-25 NIV)

To explain these verses we need to spell out the meaning of some important words: righteousness; sin; justification; redemption and sacrifice of atonement.

Righteousness – how can we be right with God?

The word righteousness, and the related idea of "being made righteous", occurs a number of times in this short passage.
But now a righteousness from God, apart from law, has been made known, to which the Law and the Prophets testify. This righteousness from God comes through faith in Jesus Christ to all who believe. (verses 21-22 in the New International Version)

But now God's way of putting people right with himself has been revealed. It has nothing to do with law, even though the Law of Moses and the prophets gave their witness to it. God puts people right through their faith in Jesus Christ. (verses 21-22 in the Good News Bible)

Righteousness is a word which carries different shades of meaning in different places in the Bible. At its heart, righteousness is that purity of character which is only fully expressed in God Himself, in God's perfect holiness, purity and justice. By nature, human beings are not righteous – our lives are spoiled by sin. By nature, we are not in a right relationship with God – we are separated from God. By ourselves, human beings can never become righteous. But Paul is talking here about a state of righteousness which comes to human beings as a gift from God. It is not a status of righteousness which anybody can earn or deserve. It does not come by obeying the Jewish Law or any other set of rules. It is not something anybody can achieve by human effort. This righteousness before God, this condition of being right with God and in a right relationship with God, is God's gift to all who put their trust in Jesus Christ.

The reason we are not righteous, and could never become righteous, is explained in the next verse.

Humanity's problem – sin

for all have sinned and fall short of the glory of God. (Romans 3:23 NIV)
For everyone has sinned; we all fall short of God's glorious standard. (verse 23 in the New Living Translation.)

Throughout his letter to the Romans, Paul explains what sin is and why sin is such a great problem for human beings. Sin makes God angry. Sin brings God's judgment. Sin separates us from God, which is spiritual death and sin also brings physical death. But what does the Bible mean by sin?

A newspaper printed a list of modern irregular verbs – words which express the same idea in different ways depending on who it is you are talking about. Here are some examples.
"I am a skilful driver, you are a reckless driver, he is a maniac behind the wheel!"
"I am generous, you are extravagant, he throws his money away."
"My children are determined, your children are wilful, his children are out of control!"

"I am prudent, you know how to take care of number one, he's a selfish so-and-so."
"I know how to express myself, you have strong opinions, he is always arguing."
"I am occasionally economical with the truth, you often bend the truth, he's a liar!"

This reminds us that there are all kinds of actions and attitudes which we know very well are wrong when we see them in other people, but when we do them we think they are acceptable. We can always justify our own actions. We see faults in other people's lives so clearly, but we turn a blind eye to these things in our own lives. The Bible has a word for all these wrong things people say and do and even think; all the selfish acts which hurt us and hurt our fellow human beings. The Bible word for these bad things we do is 'sin.'

Some people think that when Christians talk about sin they are only referring to sexual immorality. On the contrary, the Bible idea of sin includes all the bad things we do, not least the classic "seven deadly sins" of pride, jealousy, anger, gluttony, lust, laziness and greed. As somebody memorably put it, "'Sin' is just a little word with 'I' in the middle." Whenever people put 'I' in the middle of their lives, whenever they focus only on themselves and leave God out, that is what the Bible describes as sin. In our hearts, we all know what sin is and we all know that every one of us are sinners. We all know we have done and said and thought things which we should not have done. As Paul explains it to the Romans,
As it is written: "There is no-one righteous, not even one; there is no-one who understands, no-one who seeks God. All have turned away, they have together become worthless; there is no-one who does good, not even one." … for all have sinned and fall short of the glory of God. (Romans 3:10-12, 23 NIV)

If we are honest with ourselves, we all know that to be true. We have all sinned. We do all fall short of God's standard, which is perfection. And all our sins have consequences as Paul explains earlier in Romans.

Sin brings God's anger

The wrath of God is being revealed from heaven against all the godlessness and wickedness of men who suppress the truth by their wickedness, … For although they knew God, they neither glorified him as God nor gave thanks to him, but their thinking became futile and their foolish hearts were darkened. (Romans 1:18, 21)

This is the essence of sin – neither glorifying God nor giving thanks to Him. Running away from God and hiding from Him. Ignoring God and pretending he doesn't exist. These things are sin.
Since they did not think it worthwhile to retain the knowledge of God, he gave them over to a depraved mind, to do what ought not to be done. They have become filled with every kind of wickedness, evil, greed and depravity. ... they invent ways of doing evil. (Romans 1:28-29)

Here is the consequence of sin. *"God gave them over."* God gave them up. People abandoned God so God abandoned the human beings He had created. He left them alone and let them get on with their evil ways. The result is that sin cuts people off from God. Sin brings on God's anger and leads to God's judgment. Sin deserves to be punished. God is a just and holy God and judgment on sin is the inevitable expression of that justice. And sin has other effects as well.

Sin separates us from God – spiritual death

Because God is a holy God whose eyes are too pure to look on sin, human sin separates us from God who is the source of all life. That separation is spiritual and it is eternal – it is forever. Even the littlest sin cuts us off from God forever.

Sin also leads to physical death

God is the source of our human life. When sin cuts us off spiritually from God, it also limits our physical life. Sin condemns our bodies to die. From cover to cover the whole Bible is concerned with the one question of how sinful human beings can escape from the consequences of sin and the judgement of a Holy God? Because God's standard is perfection and none of us live up to that standard. The resurrection of Jesus Christ from the dead is God's warning to the whole world that the day of judgment is indeed coming.
"In the past God overlooked such ignorance, but now he commands all people everywhere to repent. For he has set a day when he will judge the world with justice by

the man he has appointed. He has given proof of this to all men by raising him from the dead." (Paul's sermon in Athens in Acts 17:30-31)

A slogan on a T-shirt asked a humorous question. "How much can I get away with and still get into heaven?" The disturbing answer is absolutely nothing. Sin makes God angry and brings divine judgment. Sin leads to spiritual death and physical death. All have sinned and fall short of the glory of God. But the good news is that God in His grace has made a way to forgive a person's sin and declare them not-guilty. When a person puts their trust in Christ God gives them a gift of righteousness: God puts them in a right relationship with Himself.

God's solution - justification

and are justified freely by his grace through the redemption that came by Christ Jesus. (Romans 3:24 NIV)
But by the free gift of God's grace all are put right with him through Christ Jesus, who sets them free. (Good News Bible)

The English word the New International Version uses for this process of being made righteous is justification. It simply means "being made just" or being made righteous. When we are justified God makes it "just as if I'd" never sinned. All are sinners. Everybody faces God's judgment. But those who put their faith in Jesus Christ are declared righteous by God. Their sins are wiped away.

The Good News Bible translates Romans 3 using different words with the same overall meaning. It translates righteousness as being in a right relationship with God. And it translates justification as being put right with God. Instead of a person being in the wrong, God treats a person as if they are in the right. Because God takes their sin away they can be in a right relationship with God.
But now God's way of putting people right with himself has been revealed. ... God puts people right through their faith in Jesus Christ. God does this to all who believe in Christ ... But by the free gift of God's grace all are put right with him through Christ Jesus, who sets them free. (Romans 3:21-22, 24)

So here is the Good News God brings us into a right relationship with Himself. And He does so by his grace which comes to us through Jesus

Christ. It is a free gift we can never earn or deserve. John Stott sums up G.R.A.C.E. as God's Riches at Christ's Expense. That freedom which Jesus has provided for us is the *"redemption which came by Christ Jesus"*.

Justification means more than pardon. Judgment would be receiving the punishment we deserve for our sins. Pardon would mean not getting the punishment we deserve. But justification means God treats us as if we had never sinned. William Barclay wrote, "To say that God justifies the ungodly means quite simply that God in his amazing love treats the sinner as if he was a good man. Again, to put it very simply, God loves us, not for anything that we are, but for what he is."

The story is told of a man who went abroad for his holidays driving his Rolls Royce. While he was there the car broke down. Understandably miffed, he phoned Rolls Royce who immediately flew one of their mechanics out. The mechanic mended the car and flew home again leaving the man to continue his holiday. But when he got home the man was worried just how much that repair was going to cost him. So he wrote a letter to Rolls Royce to ask how much he owed them. The reply came back promptly. "Dear Sir. There is no record anywhere in our files that anything has ever gone wrong with a Rolls-Royce." That is how God sees Christians once they have been put right with him, once they have been justified. As if nothing had ever gone wrong.

Now let's unpack this wonderful redemption. Just exactly what has God done which sets us free? Christians answer this question in slightly different ways, but all agree that God's way of salvation is all wrapped up in the death and resurrection of Jesus Christ.

Christ's death on the cross

God presented him as a sacrifice of atonement, through faith in his blood. (Romans 3:25 NIV)
God offered him, so that by his blood he should become the means by which people's sins are forgiven through their faith in him. (Good News Bible)
God sent him to die in our place to take away our sins. We receive forgiveness through faith in the blood of Jesus' death. (New Century Version)

For God presented Jesus as the sacrifice for sin. People are made right with God when they believe that Jesus sacrificed his life, shedding his blood. (New Living Translation.)

Our forgiveness comes at a terrible price – the death of Jesus on the cross. That event was not the execution of a common criminal. The Bible tells us that Jesus's death had a spiritual and indeed a cosmic significance. Christ's death was unique because Jesus Christ was unique in at least two ways. Jesus was unique because he was more than a man. Jesus was also the Son of God, God Himself born as a human being. And Jesus was also unique because He was completely innocent. He had never done anything wrong. He was without sin. He had never done anything to make God angry. There was nothing in Jesus's life separating Him from God. He did not deserve any punishment. He had no sin which would cause him to die, spiritually or physically.

Since Jesus was innocent. he did not die because of His own sins – he had no sin. Jesus's death was a sacrifice for sin in the same sense as in the Old Testament so many lambs were sacrificed. As John the Baptist said when He first saw Jesus, *"Behold the Lamb of God who takes away the sins of the world."* (John 1:29)
For Christ died for sins once for all, the righteous for the unrighteous, to bring you to God. (1 Peter 3:18)

Jesus's death was a sacrifice of atonement, paying the penalty for sin. Atonement could be rewritten 'at-one-ment'. Jesus's death brings us back to God and makes us one with God again. And all we need to do is receive by faith what Christ's death in our place has bought for us. The story is told of an evangelist who had just finished his open air preaching service and was about to leave when a young man approached him and asked, "What must I do to be saved?" The evangelist replied. "It's too late!" The inquirer was disappointed. "Don't say that!" But the evangelist insisted, "It's too late!" "You want to know what you have to do to be saved. It's too late. The work of salvation is done, completed, finished! It was finished on the cross. You can't do anything. Except receive as a gift by faith what Christ has already accomplished."

Through the life, death and resurrection of Jesus Christ, God has made a way for us to be saved, for our sins to be forgiven, for us to be put into a right relationship with God and to receive God's completely free gift of eternal life. Our next chapter answers the vital question: how should we respond to God's love? What must we do to begin to experience this wonderful relationship with God?

4 How should we respond to the Good News?

I am not ashamed of the gospel, because it is the power of God for the salvation of everyone who believes: first for the Jew, then for the Gentile. For in the gospel a righteousness from God is revealed, a righteousness that is by faith from first to last. (Romans 1:16-17)

The word gospel simply means 'Good News'. We find it more than 75 times in the New Testament meaning 'the message of good news': the good news about Jesus. It is this message of Good News which leads men and women to all the blessings of salvation as we receive and believe that message.

The old question, "are you saved?", sounds dated. But it is still perhaps the most important question for anybody to answer. We do still all need to be saved. The gospel is God's power bringing salvation to all who believe – to everyone who puts their trust in Jesus. It is a simple straightforward message which can transform each of our lives.

The apostle Paul unwraps the gospel at the beginning of his letter to the Roman Christians like this.
Paul, a servant of Christ Jesus, called to be an apostle and set apart for the gospel of God – the gospel he promised beforehand through his prophets in the Holy Scriptures regarding his Son, who as to his human nature was a descendant of David, and who through the Spirit of holiness was declared with power to be the Son of God by his resurrection from the dead: Jesus Christ our Lord. (Romans 1:1-4)

This tells us that the Good News comes from God: it is *the gospel of God.* And the Bible contains the Good News *promised beforehand through his prophets in the Holy Scriptures.* The gospel was the culmination of God's masterplan of salvation which unfolded over thousands of years as recorded in the Scriptures, God's word, the Bible. In the Old Testament the story of the Exodus tells us how God rescued his people out of slavery in Egypt across the red sea and eventually to the promised land. This gives us a picture of the salvation God had prepared since before the Creation of the World. When the time was right all the promises had God made to Abraham and Isaac and Jacob and through the Prophets like Isaiah and Jeremiah would all be fulfilled in Jesus. So we find the gospel itself revealed in the second portion of the Bible, the New Testament. This Good News is all wrapped up in the life and death and resurrection of the Son of God, Jesus Christ.

Jesus is the Son of God, *regarding his Son, who as to his human nature was a descendant of David.* This is the message of Christmas. Jesus was a man, fully human, descended from David, the greatest King Israel ever knew. But at the same time Jesus was also the Son of God, fully God yet born as an ordinary human being.

Then also, Jesus is still alive, *declared with power to be the Son of God by his resurrection from the dead.* This is the revolutionary message of Easter. Jesus was dead – and now He is alive again! The resurrection is God's proof that Jesus is indeed the Son of God. Jesus was more than a human being: He was also the Son of God. And the proof we have that Jesus really was the Son of God is that God raised his Son Jesus from the dead. The resurrection is God's proof to everybody of who Jesus really is. The historical fact that God raised Jesus from the dead is central to the gospel and is so important that we will devote the next chapter to it.

Before we go on, we should recall the other important part of the Easter story and the gospel message which we considered in chapter 3. That is the death of Jesus on the cross. Jesus looked ahead to his death on the cross when he said, *"For even the Son of Man did not come to be served, but to serve, and to give his life as a ransom for many.*" (Mark 10:45) Jesus died in our place so that we can be forgiven. There are different ways to understand what was actually happening as Jesus died on the cross but all agree that the death of Jesus was an essential element in God's plan of salvation. So Jesus is the Son of God – His resurrection from the dead proves that. The Message Translation puts it this way: *His descent from David roots him in history; his unique identity as Son of God was shown by the Spirit when Jesus was raised from the dead, setting him apart as the Messiah, our Master.* (Romans 1:3-4)

And this points us to the core of the Gospel – *Jesus Christ our Lord.* That is the core of the Good News which turns the world upside down; the simple announcement, "Jesus is Lord." Paul quoted a hymn from the Early Church in his letter to the Colossians.
(Christ) is the image of the invisible God, the firstborn over all creation. For by him all things were created: things in heaven and on earth, visible and invisible, whether

thrones or powers or rulers or authorities; all things were created by him and for him. He is before all things, and in him all things hold together. (Colossians 1:15-17)

Christians believe that Jesus is Lord because of who He is in Himself – the Son of God. And Jesus is also Lord because of what He has done in the act of creating everything that exists. Everything was created by Him and for Him and He holds everything together. Somebody has said, "There is not one square inch of the entire creation about which Jesus Christ does not declare, 'This is mine! This belongs to me!'" And then one event in history reveals to the world just how important Jesus is. That was His resurrection from the dead. We know that Jesus is Lord because God raised Him from the dead. The resurrection is God's demonstration to the whole universe that Jesus Christ is Lord of all.

In the New Testament that simple declaration that "Jesus is Lord" is sufficient to demonstrate that a person is actually a believer. A true Christian is somebody who recognises and declares that Jesus Christ is Lord. It may seem to us that saying "Jesus is Lord" is no big deal. But the New Testament was written in the days of the Roman Empire, particularly in the times of Emperors like Nero who cruelly persecuted the church and brutally murdered thousands of Christians. In those days, refusing to acknowledge "Caesar is Lord" and insisting instead that the only Lord is the Lord Jesus Christ really was a very big deal. Proclaiming "Jesus is Lord" was like declaring war. It was a cry of revolution. It was no less controversial and radical than standing up in Nazi Germany and saying, "Hitler is not Fuhrer, Jesus is in charge." In the universe of Star Wars, it would be like saying, "The Emperor is not in charge, Luke Skywalker is."

So what does it really mean to declare that Jesus is Lord? Consider some other titles we could use instead of Lord to make the meaning clear. In the Roman Empire in the First Century slaves had their Master. In the world of work today we could talk about the Boss, the Manager, the Supervisor, the Director, the Controller. The person who tells you what to do. The military use labels like Chief, Leader, even Supreme Commander. Even more than at work, in the armed forces the commanding officer gives instructions and you obey. The world of politics has a whole range of titles for the person in ultimate charge. Emperor; Ruler; Sovereign; Monarch; King; Tsar; President; Premier.

With all of these people, you do what they say. They are in charge. They lead, you follow. They tell you what to do and they tell you what not to do. And you don't argue. You obey. That is what it means to declare, "Jesus is Lord." Jesus Christ is King of Kings and Lord of Lords. He is our Master. So much more important than any political or military leader. So much more important than any boss. We do what Jesus says. We go where he goes. We follow Jesus without reservation, without qualification, without hesitation. Because Jesus is Lord. This simple statement is the core of the gospel.

Let us be clear: Jesus is not Lord because people allow Him to be Lord. Jesus is not Lord because people have voted for Him to be Lord. Jesus is Lord because Almighty God has said it is so. It is a fact and the different opinions people might have about that fact do not change anything. Jesus Christ is Lord of all. Fact. It does not make any difference whether a person believes Jesus is Lord or chooses not to believe Jesus is Lord or even if they don't know that Jesus is Lord. The Lordship of Christ is like gravity. It is a fact. Gravity isn't affected by whether we believe in it or not. If we are sensible we will recognise that gravity exists and has a claim on our lives. From time to time some people try to live as if gravity doesn't exist. They jump out of planes and for a few seconds pretend they are completely free of any pull gravity might have on them. But gravity has a way of bringing everybody down to earth with a bump sooner or later. The Bible tells us that sooner or later everybody will recognise that Jesus is Lord whether they have chosen to accept Him or even if they have devoted their lives to rejecting Him. Jesus is Lord. Fact.

So, with all the implications we have just talked about, that simple statement "Jesus is Lord" is the heart of the Good News. The gospel is an announcement. But at the same time it is not just information. It is also an invitation and a challenge. So how should people respond to this Good News? What must a person do to receive God's free gift of forgiveness and eternal life and begin to enjoy a personal relationship with God as Father?

If you confess with your mouth, "Jesus is Lord," and believe in your heart that God raised him from the dead, you will be saved. For it is with your heart that you believe and are justified, and it is with your mouth that you confess and are saved. As the

Scripture says, "Anyone who trusts in him will never be put to shame." (Romans 10:9-11)

In order to experience salvation, we simply need to put our trust in God. Faith is the channel by which God's blessing comes to us. This is not saying that we earn our salvation by putting our trust in God. Faith is not some kind of good work we have to do to deserve God's love. We never could earn or deserve God's grace. But we receive God's free gift of eternal life simply by believing God's promises and accepting them for ourselves.

If we really believe the Good News of Jesus, our faith will be much more than an intellectual agreement to the truth of certain facts. Faith is a commitment to trusting God which affects every part of our lives. In June of 1859 the legendary tightrope walker Charles Blondin strung a rope 340 metres long at a height of 50 metres above the waters of Niagara Falls. After walking across he then walked back and paused half way to cook and eat an omelette. Blondin crossed with his manager Harry Colcord on his back. Then he crossed Niagara Falls once more pushing a wheelbarrow. The story goes (although it may only be a myth) that Blondin then asked the cheering crowds, "Who believes I can carry a person across in the wheelbarrow?" Lots of people agreed that he would be able to do that. "Right", said Blondin, "If you believe I can do that, get in the wheelbarrow!" Faith in Jesus is not merely believing he can save me, but putting my life into his hands. It means getting into the wheelbarrow. In F.A.I.T.H., "Facts lead to Actions when I Trust in my Heart."

Believing in our hearts, the Bible says in Romans 10:9-11, will always be accompanied by confessing with our mouths that Jesus Christ is Lord. Christians are obliged to express our faith in words and declare in public our allegiance to Jesus Christ as Lord. There is no such thing as a secret disciple. Either the secret will destroy our discipleship or our discipleship will destroy the secret. Believe and also confess.

From the very beginning of His ministry, Jesus demanded a very similar response from His followers. *Jesus came to Galilee, proclaiming the good news of God, and saying, "The time is fulfilled, and the kingdom of God has come near; repent, and believe in the good news."* (Mark 1:14-15)

We have thought about what it means to "believe the Good News". Alongside putting our trust in God, Jesus called for people to repent. *Repent and believe.* Repentance is an important idea for everyone who wants to follow Jesus Christ. At its root the word means a complete change of direction. To do a U-turn in life. If anybody wants to meet God, they have to change direction. If we have our back to the light, all we can see is the darkness of our own shadow. If we want to see the light, we have to turn around and walk towards it.

The starting point in the process of repentance is recognising the problem of sin which separates us from God. We need to accept that there are things in our lives which need to change. All the things we do and say and think which hurt other people and actually hurt ourselves most of all: all the things we would love to change about our lives if only we could. To use a phrase from the Church of England Book of Common Prayer, we need to "acknowledge and bewail our manifold sins and wickedness". We need to be truly sorry for our sins. Then we need to confess those sins before God and ask his forgiveness, for the times we sin against God and against our neighbours, through ignorance, through weakness, but most of the time through our own deliberate fault.

There is a story about Frederick II who was King of Prussia back in the eighteenth-century. One day the King went to inspect the prison in Berlin. The prisoners all fell on their knees protesting their unjust imprisonment. There were endless tales of innocence, of misunderstood motives, and of exploitation. While listening to these pleas of innocence, Frederick's eye was caught by a solitary figure in the corner, a prisoner who seemed unconcerned with all the commotion.
"Why are you here?" Frederick asked him.
"Armed robbery, Your Majesty."
"Well," remarked the King, "I suppose you are an innocent victim too? Were you guilty?"
"Oh yes, indeed, Your Majesty. I entirely deserve my punishment." At that Frederick summoned the jailer. "Release this guilty man at once," he said. "Before he corrupts all these fine innocent people in here!"

Repentance means admitting our sins. But more than that, repentance means being sorry enough for our sins that we are ready to give them up and ask God to change us. The Good News Bible translates Jesus's call to repent as *"turn away from your sins."* The Message Translation is *"change your life."* Repent: acknowledge your sins, confess them and change your ways. The New Testament was written down in Greek and that language has two ways of giving commands. One would be the one-off event, repent just once. But the word Jesus used commands an action which is repeated. It means repent lots of times, not just once but keep on repenting. The first act of repentance is only the beginning. Just as we need to keep on putting our trust in God, so also we need to keep on turning our lives round, to keep on saying no to sin and yes to God.

God offers each and every one of us this amazing gift of forgiveness and new life. He promises to change us from enemies into friends, to welcome us as precious sons and daughters. By his grace, God will put us back in a right relationship with Himself on the basis of Christ's death and resurrection. The gospel offers us that gift of righteousness and all the blessings of salvation and it is *the power of God for the salvation of all who believe*. And we receive God's free gift when we obey Jesus's command to *repent and believe*. When we believe enough to get into the wheelbarrow. When we change direction in life and as we *confess with our mouths* to the watching world that Jesus Christ is indeed Lord of all.

5 Didn't he used to be dead?

"What makes you believe that God exists?" "Is Jesus the only way to God?" For these questions, as in many other conversations we may have about Jesus, there is one thing Christians will want to talk about. That is the glorious resurrection of the Lord Jesus Christ from the dead. The resurrection is clearly the most important evidence for the existence of God. At the same time the resurrection is the historical event which sets Jesus Christ apart from all other religious figures and demonstrates the uniqueness both of Christ and of the Christian faith. Didn't he used to be dead?

The resurrection of Jesus is at the heart of our Christian belief. This was the content of the good news which the first disciples preached: Jesus is risen from the dead and we have seen Him! (Acts 2:32; Acts 3:15; Acts 4:10). It was an encounter with the Risen Christ which transformed the enemy of the church Saul into the Apostle Paul. The resurrection was at the heart of the creed of the Early Church (1 Corinthians 15:3-8) and the ultimate proof that Jesus Christ is indeed Lord of all. The resurrection is integral to that most simple confession of faith which we talked about in the last chapter.

If you confess with your mouth, "Jesus is Lord," and believe in your heart that God raised him from the dead, you will be saved. For it is with your heart that you believe and are justified, and it is with your mouth that you confess and are saved.
(Romans 10:9-10)

It follows that Christians will want to be able to defend our conviction that Jesus Christ rose from the dead. There are at least four strands of evidence we can point to.

The empty tomb

We can start with the fact that Jesus was buried on Good Friday but when his disciples went to the tomb on that first Easter Sunday morning the tomb was empty and the body of Jesus had disappeared. The evidence that the tomb was empty is conclusive. The burial site was known to disciples, to the Jews and to the Roman authorities alike. If any of His opponents knew where the body of Jesus had gone, they would have said so. No alternative theory for the disappearance of Jesus's body holds water. The first Jewish response to claims of the resurrection, "the disciples stole the body," is recorded in Matthew chapter 28 and that presupposes the fact that the tomb was actually empty. The empty tomb was discovered by women who in those times would be viewed as very unreliable witnesses and that makes it highly implausible that the story of the empty tomb was invented.

The gospel accounts of the resurrection are based on earlier accounts which may have been written or may equally have been passed on mouth-to-mouth. Either would have been reliable and must have originated within only a few years of Jesus's death, as were the many mentions of the resurrection in the New Testament Letters. The four gospels contain different accounts of the resurrection and the Longer Ending of Mark (Mark 16:9-20) then makes a fifth account all telling a similar story but with enough differences to imply independent witnesses. D. H. van Daalen has pointed out, "It is extremely difficult to object to the empty tomb on historical grounds; those who deny it do so on the basis of theological or philosophical assumptions."

The resurrection appearances

We can then talk about the appearances of Jesus to His disciples after his resurrection.
For what I received I passed on to you as of first importance: that Christ died for our sins according to the Scriptures, that he was buried, that he was raised on the third day according to the Scriptures, and that he appeared to Peter, and then to the Twelve. After that, he appeared to more than five hundred of the brothers at the same time, most of whom are still living, though some have fallen asleep. Then he appeared to James, then to all the apostles, and last of all he appeared to me also.
(1 Corinthians 15:3-8)

This catalogue of resurrection appearances is generally believed to be a pre-existing Christian tradition which Paul heard from the Jerusalem apostles early in his ministry. That would date it to within five years of the death of Christ. Many of those named eyewitnesses to the resurrection were certainly still alive when Paul wrote and the combined impact of their testimony cannot be dismissed as mere 'legend.' New Testament scholar Norman Perrin wrote, "The more we study the tradition with regard to the appearances, the firmer the rock begins to appear upon which they are based."

The growth of the church and the Christian faith

Defending the historical event of the resurrection, we can go on to point to the origins and the growth of the church and of the Christian faith. William Lane Craig wrote, "Without belief in Jesus' resurrection, Christianity could never have come into being. The crucifixion would have remained the final tragedy in the hapless life of Jesus. The origin of Christianity hinges on the belief of these earliest disciples that Jesus had risen from the dead." There were no beliefs around before the life of Christ which could have been the source of the idea of Jesus's resurrection. Some Jews understood the resurrection of the dead as something which would happen after the end of the world, but not during human history, and for all of God's people, not just for one individual. The only coherent explanation for the emergence of the belief in the resurrection and the consequent expansion of the church is that Jesus did indeed rise from the dead. As C.F.D. Moule wrote:

> "If the coming into existence of the Nazarenes, a phenomenon undeniably attested by the New Testament, rips a great hole in history, a hole of the size and shape of the Resurrection, what does the secular historian propose to stop it up with? … the birth and rapid rise of the Christian Church … *remain an unsolved enigma for any historian who refuses to take seriously the only explanation offered by the church itself."*

All the evidence points to the amazing truth that Jesus did indeed rise from the dead. The popular notion that the disciples stole the body and invented the story of the resurrection is unconvincing. Honest men seeking to invent a religion which prizes truth so highly would not build its whole foundation on a lie. A group of people who had seen their leader crucified and were terrified they would be next would not suddenly start preaching and even be martyred for insisting that that Jesus was alive if they knew that was untrue. The only credible explanation for the dramatic change in the lives of all the disciples is that Jesus had indeed risen from the dead. It is equally unrealistic to suggest that Jesus did not actually die on the cross but merely swooned and then woke up in the tomb, or to suggest that all the disciples experienced hallucinations.

Sherlock Holmes made the point well. "When you have eliminated the impossible, whatever remains, however improbable, must be the truth." Didn't he used to be dead?

The changed lives of Christians today

In this post-modern post-Christendom world people are not always persuaded by historical facts. As well as being able to produce evidence for the historicity of the resurrection it is also appropriate for us to point to other kinds of evidence that Jesus Christ is alive. Christians should not be afraid of talking about our own experiences of Jesus, the differences Jesus makes in our own lives and that we have seen Jesus make in the lives of other people. We can talk about answers to prayer and experiences of healing and peace and joy and guidance. From our own personal experiences, Christians have very good reasons to believe that Jesus Christ is truly risen from the dead and is alive with us today.

The theologian Wolfhart Pannenberg said this. "The evidence for Jesus's resurrection is so strong that nobody would question it except for two things. First, it is a very unusual event. And second, if you believe it happened, you have to change the way you live." Christians can talk about the evidence for the empty tomb, the resurrection appearances, the spectacular rise of the early church and the difference the Risen Christ has made in the lives of Christians through history and even in our own lives. Separately and together these point to the historical event when Jesus Christ rose from the dead. The resurrection is the cornerstone of our faith. It proves that the claims Jesus made about Himself were true. The resurrection also gives us good reason to believe that the rest of the Bible is true and equally to believe that the God of the Bible exists. The resurrection points to the uniqueness of Christ and the uniqueness of the Christian faith which confirms the claim Jesus made, *"No-one comes to the Father except by me."* (John 14:6) The resurrection is God's warning to humanity of impending judgment (Acts 17:31). At the same time in the face of post-modern pessimism regarding life beyond death, the resurrection of Jesus Christ gives us the grounds of a genuine hope of eternal life. Because He lives we will live also! This is the Good News Christians have been given to share. Didn't he used to be dead?

6 What makes you believe that God exists?

One of the most important questions folk might ask about the Christian faith is this. "What makes us believe there is a God, or that we can get to know that God?"

Many people question whether there is a God or not. Not so many are actually convinced that there is no God although some do think that way. In the Bible Psalm 14:1 and Psalm 53:1 both say, *"The fool says, in his heart, 'There is no God.'"* Nowadays people who say that write books about it and are even given their own television shows. But the truth is that anybody who confidently declares "there is no God" as if that was a proven fact is indeed foolish. They are making a fundamental mistake. It makes no sense to categorically deny the existence of God who is generally unseen even by those who do believe He exists. It is not meaningful to say that something which possibly could exist absolutely does not exist. All anyone can reliably say is, "if there is a God I haven't seen evidence of his existence yet." People who say "God does not exist" are only expressing their own personal belief. Someone who declares that God cannot possibly exist is making the same mistake as someone who insists that Australia cannot possibly exist, just because they haven't personally been there yet. They are being as foolish as people would be if they said, "the Queen doesn't exist", because they have never met Her Majesty, and refuse to believe the photographs or the Christmas broadcasts or all the people who claim that they have met the Queen.

The science fiction author Isaac Asimov made the same mistake as very many people. He wrote, "I am an atheist, out and out. I don't have the evidence to prove that God doesn't exist, but I so strongly suspect he does not that I don't want to waste my time." Asimov had closed his mind to the evidence for God's existence, so in the end he was not able to see what many others can. But Christians have seen that evidence of God. We have experienced the power of God and seen Him at work. As a teenager I used to argue vigorously that God couldn't exist. Then God showed me that I had been wrong!

The way we all see the world, our "world view", depends on where we are standing; where we are coming from. A simple story illustrates this

truth. Two people were walking along a river bank one day when they saw a man across the river.
"How can we get across?" they shouted.
"Why would you be wanting to do that then?" the man asked.
"We want to get to the other side," they explained patiently.
"Don't be daft," the man replied. "You're already on the other side."

What we see depends on where we are standing, on our frames of reference and our "world view". And we will not always interpret what we see correctly. Our interpretations can be distorted by our presuppositions, our preconceived ideas, the things we assume and take for granted. A mind which is closed to God may not see God. But a mind which is open to spiritual things can recognise evidence for the existence of God.

Hebrews 11:6 tells us, *"Without faith it is impossible to please God, because anyone who comes to him must believe that he exists and that he rewards those who earnestly seek him."*

When Christians and seekers look around the world with the eye of faith, evidence for God's existence is everywhere. Here are four areas which we can point to as evidence for the existence of God, in order of increasing importance. To begin with, we might point to the Bible and to the Church.

The Bible and the Church

Some people are struck by the impact and the uniqueness of the Bible. Most people who say "the Bible isn't true" actually haven't read the Bible. So Christians can encourage our friends to open the Bible, starting with the Gospels, and rely on God speaking to them through His word. Spurgeon said, "Defend the Bible? I would as soon defend a lion! Unchain it and it will defend itself." We need to unchain the lion and encourage our friends to read the Bible.

We can also talk about the historical impact of the church on the world, and the influence of Christianity on society today. We can point to all the good things Christians have done and are doing in caring for the poor and working for justice and peace, from William Booth and Lord

Shaftsbury to Martin Luther King, Mother Teresa and Archbishop Desmond Tutu, from Food Banks and homeless shelters and support for refugees to Christian Aid and Operation Christmas Child. All these things point beyond the individuals to the Living God working through them. Next we can point to the many ways God has revealed Himself in Creation.

Creation

The heavens declare the glory of God; the skies proclaim the work of his hands.
Day after day they pour forth speech; night after night they display knowledge.
There is no speech or language where their voice is not heard.
Their voice goes out into all the earth, their words to the ends of the world.
(Psalm 19:1-4)

God has revealed Himself to the world in all He has created.
What may be known about God is plain to them, because God has made it plain to them. For since the creation of the world God's invisible qualities—his eternal power and divine nature—have been clearly seen, being understood from what has been made, so that men are without excuse. (Romans 1:19-20)

So the Bible tells us that God's eternal power and His divine nature can clearly be seen in the world around. There are many different aspects of the created world which reveal God if we look at them with open minds. We can point to beauty and majesty in Creation; sunsets and starry skies, waterfalls and flowers. It was the French biologist Louis Pasteur who said, "Posterity will someday laugh at the foolishness of our modern materialistic philosophy. The more I study nature the more I am amazed at the Creator."

Those of a more scientific mind may appreciate the beauty inherent in mathematics and physics. The way creation works is marvellous to unravel. The Twentieth Century British physicist Paul Dirac once said, "it is more important to have beauty in one's equations that to have them fit experiment." We can point to evidence of design in Creation. Physicists talk about the "fine tuning of the universe", the way that the laws of physics, the rate of expansion of the universe and the values of the fundamental constants all fit together in exactly the right balance to make life possible. If any of those were slightly different, no life could exist.

From atoms to astrophysics, all this is evidence of design in the natural world, and design points beyond itself to the Designer. Biologists can point to the way eyes work, and memory and thinking in the human brain, and the complex interactions of DNA and RNA and dozens of separate proteins in the process of inheritance, which cannot take place if even one ingredient in the process is absent.

Looking at human beings, we can talk about the wonder of human language. There is the aesthetic aspect of our personality: we can appreciate and create beautiful art and inspiring music. Then we can point to the universal spiritual experience of human beings. We are the only animals that pray or worship. When we answered the question, "What is the point of life?" we spoke about the "God shaped gap" in our lives. As Augustine said back in the fifth century, "You have made us for yourself, O Lord, and our hearts are restless until they rest in you."

Another common experience of all human beings is conscience: the ability to distinguish right from wrong and good from evil. Morality and ethics are consequences of us all being created in the image of the holy and righteous God.

Indeed, when Gentiles, who do not have the law, do by nature things required by the law, they are a law for themselves, even though they do not have the law, since they show that the requirements of the law are written on their hearts, their consciences also bearing witness, and their thoughts now accusing, now even defending them.
(Romans 2:14-15)

Mark Twain put it this way. "Man is the only animal that blushes. Or needs to." Our human conscience is evidence for the existence of God. We will explore the idea of "the image of God" in human beings further in the next chapter.

Finally, looking at creation, one of the classic 'proofs' of the existence of God is called the 'cosmological argument.' Once there was nothing, no space, no time, no matter, nothing. Then there was something. The universe came from nothing – something came from nothing and life came from not life and that requires a First Cause, a First Mover, something which started the whole thing off. And that First Cause was God. None of these pieces of evidence in creation for the existence of God are irrefutable knock-down proof that God does exist. But together they do give us very strong grounds to claim that believing in God is reasonable and rational. J. B. Phillips wrote, "God is not discoverable or demonstrable by purely scientific means, unfortunately for the scientifically-minded. But that really proves nothing. It simply means that the wrong instruments are being used for the job."

The changed lives of Christians

We can point to evidence for God's existence in human experience. Christians can point to the changed lives of the first disciples. One day they were hiding away terrified that they would be next to be crucified. The next day these ordinary men and women were preaching a message which would turn the world upside down. We can point to countless inspirational Christians through the ages. We can talk about Christians we have read and heard about and even better we can give specific examples of the differences we have seen Jesus make in the lives of people we know. Best of all we can talk about our own personal experiences of the ways God has worked in our own lives: answers to prayer; miracles of grace and of healing; experiences of peace and joy and forgiveness. We are certain that God exists because we have experienced Jesus in our own lives. And then, most importantly, we know God exists because of Jesus himself.

Jesus Christ

Michael Green wrote, "One of the greatest tragedies in the ossifying Western church is that people do not, by and large, talk about Jesus. That is extremely foolish. Jesus is the supremely attractive one. If we exclude from our conversations the only really winning card that we have, we are of all people most to be pitied."[1]

Christians can point to the uniqueness of Jesus. His birth, his teaching, his ministry and his death on the cross all set him apart from all the other leaders of all the other religions. We will talk more about this in chapter 9. We can point our friends to the love Jesus showed and to his perfect character. And we can discuss the teaching of Jesus.

---

[1] Michael Green *Evangelism Through the Local Church* Hodder 1990 88.

Jesus answered, "I am the way and the truth and the life. No one comes to the Father except through me. If you really knew me, you would know my Father as well. From now on, you do know him and have seen him."
Philip said, "Lord, show us the Father and that will be enough for us."
Jesus answered: "Don't you know me, Philip, even after I have been among you such a long time? Anyone who has seen me has seen the Father. (John 14:6-9)

Anyone who has seen me has seen the Father, Jesus said. First and foremost, Christians know that God exists and we believe in God because we have met God in His Son Jesus Christ. And in all of this the supreme evidence for God's existence is found in the one historical event we thought about in the last chapter, the Resurrection of Jesus from the dead. Everything rests on the resurrection of Jesus. That was the heart of the gospel the first Christians preached and it is the heart of our gospel today. Jesus is not dead. Jesus is alive! The resurrection is God's proof that everything that Jesus claimed about Himself is true. It is God's proof that Jesus is the Son of God and that Jesus is indeed King of Kings and Lord of Lords. And the historical fact of the resurrection is the ultimate proof that God exists. The resurrection is that important.

I am sure you have seen optical illusions of pictures which can be viewed two ways. "Rubin's Vase" appears to be a pair of faces in silhouette looking at each other. But look again and the middle of the picture looks like a vase. Or there is another famous picture which can appear to be of a young lady but looked at again appears to be an old lady instead. Our eyes see the one picture but our brains are able to interpret the same image in different ways. It is the same when people look at the world around us: the beauty of a sunset, the majesty of the night sky and the intricacy of flowers. Or the amazing ways which the human eye or brain work, or the complex interplay of proteins and DNA in the mechanism of inheritance. Some people look at these things and interpret them as examples of design in Creation and evidence for the existence of God. Other people look at exactly the same things but do not see God anywhere. When people look at those kinds of optical illusions, whichever picture they may see first they can usually see the other interpretation after a while as well. Then they will be able to switch mentally between one image and the other. In the same way people who may never have seen the hand of God in the world around before can begin to see God in his Creation, or in the lives of other people. And

people can come to see Jesus in a completely new light too, not as a long dead figure from history but as the Son of God, risen from the dead to be our Saviour. This kind of change, seeing the world in a dramatically new way, is part of what Jesus meant when he said,
"I tell you the truth, no one can see the kingdom of God unless he is born again. …. Flesh gives birth to flesh, but the Spirit gives birth to spirit. 'You must be born again.'" (John 3:3, 5-7)

God has revealed Himself in the Bible and in the church, and in Creation. God has revealed Himself in human experience, the experiences of other people and our own personal experiences. But ultimately we believe in God because of Jesus and supremely because of the resurrection. Jesus is alive! That is the good news Christians are given to share.

7. Just how did God create the world?

In the Bible, the Fourth of the Ten Commandments says, *"In six days the* L*ORD made the heavens and the earth, the sea, and all that is in them,"* (Exodus 20:11). In our modern scientific world, what does that mean? What do Christians actually believe about how God created the world?

There are basically three common ideas around about how the world came to exist; one comes from science, the other two come from the Christian faith. Many people assume that science has proved that everything came into existence by natural processes and random chance. From the subtle unchallenged assumption of evolution in David Attenborough's natural history films, to the explicit anti-theism of Richard Dawkins and Steve Jones, the impression is given everywhere that all scientists reject the idea of a Creator.

This assumption that science has proved God cannot exist is only that – an assumption. As we discussed in the last chapter, science has not and indeed never will be able to prove that God does not exist. And scientific understandings of how the universe came into existence and how life began are theories, not proven facts. The minds of some scientists are closed to the idea of God as Creator so in the end they can't see the evidence for God's existence which Christians do see. We have experienced the power of God and seen him at work. It was Albert Einstein who said "Science without religion is blind. Religion without science is lame." The truth is that science will never prove decisively whether God created everything or not. Knowing God as creator is a matter of faith not science. We will develop this point below.

We need a 'change of mind' if we are ever going to see God.

As we thought earlier, what we see depends on our point of view, on where we are standing to begin with. Many people are blinded by the way the media suggests that science has replaced God. As a result they simply cannot see God. Some scientists are so locked into their way of looking at the world that they genuinely cannot see the evidence for God which is all around them. But for anyone who looks for it with the eye of faith, that evidence is plain to see. Scientists, as much as anybody else, just need to switch their way of looking at the world – to move from a view of the world which excludes God to a view of the world which allows the possibility of God in it.

In contrast to scientists, Christians (and Jews and Muslims and people of all faiths) believe that God created the whole universe. All Christians believe that God created the universe. The fourth century declaration of Christian faith the Nicene Creed begins, "I believe in one God, the Father Almighty, Maker of heaven and earth, and of all things visible and invisible." From beginning to end the Bible teaches is that God is the Creator. God created space and time, matter and energy, all things out of nothing. More than that, God then designed and formed and shaped everything into the way we see things today.

The first three chapters of the first book of the Bible, Genesis, give accounts of God creating the universe. Then the Old Testament describes God as Creator in so many other places as well. In Exodus 20 when God gives the Ten Commandments to Moses and Israel, the fact that God is Creator is given as the reason behind the Fourth Commandment.

"Remember the Sabbath day by keeping it holy. Six days you shall labor and do all your work, but the seventh day is a Sabbath to the LORD *your God. On it you shall not do any work, ... For in six days the* LORD *made the heavens and the earth, the sea, and all that is in them, but he rested on the seventh day. Therefore the* LORD *blessed the Sabbath day and made it holy.* (Exodus 20:8-11)

So the distinctive Jewish pattern which Christians then adopted of setting apart one day each week as special to honour God was originally given as a weekly reminder that God is Creator of all things.

Throughout the Psalms God is worshipped as Creator, for example in Psalm 89:11, Psalm 104:5, Psalm 148 especially verses 5-6. Like most of the Prophets, Isaiah sees God as Creator of Heaven and Earth (e.g. Isaiah 42:5, 45:12). We read God's own words in Isaiah chapter 40.

"Who has measured the waters in the hollow of his hand, or with the breadth of his hand marked off the heavens? Who has held the dust of the earth in a basket, or weighed the mountains on the scales and the hills in a balance? .....

He sits enthroned above the circle of the earth, and its people are like grasshoppers. He stretches out the heavens like a canopy, and spreads them out like a tent to live in. ...

"To whom will you compare me? Or who is my equal?" says the Holy One. Lift your eyes and look to the heavens: Who created all these? He who brings out the starry host one by one, and calls them each by name. Because of his great power and mighty strength, not one of them is missing. ….
Do you not know? Have you not heard? The LORD is the everlasting God, the Creator of the ends of the earth." (Isaiah 40:12, 22, 25-26, 28)

The whole of the New Testament assumes that God created everything. Jesus speaks about God as Creator in Mark 10:6 and Mark 13:19. Among the letters, 1 Corinthians, Ephesians, Colossians, 1 Timothy, James, 1 Peter and Hebrews speak of God as Creator. The picture of worship in heaven in Revelation chapter 4 includes these words:
"Holy, holy, holy is the Lord God Almighty, who was, and is, and is to come." …
"You are worthy, our Lord and God, to receive glory and honour and power, for you created all things, and by your will they were created and have their being."
(Revelation 4:8,11)

In the New Testament Jesus Christ himself is named as the Creator.

In the beginning was the Word (referring to Jesus), *and the Word was with God, and the Word was God. He was with God in the beginning. Through him all things were made; without him nothing was made that has been made.* (John 1:1-3)

(Christ) is the image of the invisible God, the firstborn over all creation. For by him all things were created: things in heaven and on earth, visible and invisible, whether thrones or powers or rulers or authorities; all things were created by him and for him. He is before all things, and in him all things hold together. (Colossians 1:15-17)

In the past God spoke to our forefathers through the prophets at many times and in various ways, but in these last days he has spoken to us by his Son, whom he appointed heir of all things, and through whom he made the universe.
(Hebrews 1:1-2)

One verse in the letter to the Hebrews sums up two important aspects of the Christian understanding of Creation. *By faith we understand that the universe was formed at God's command, so that what is seen was not made out of what was visible.* (Hebrews 11:3)

Looking at the second half of the verse first, Christians understand creation to be creation from nothing, what philosophers with their love of Latin call creation *"ex nihilo"*. If God had merely shaped what now exists from 'stuff' which had already existed that would be termed creation *"ex materia"*. But God's work in creation was not merely to shape already existing 'stuff' into the forms it now takes. Hebrews 11:3 tells us, *"By faith we understand … that what is seen was not made out of what was visible."* God did not just shape things from what already existed. When Christians say God is Creator, we mean that God made absolutely everything that exists. God did not just create all the matter and all the energy in the universe. God created the universe. Before that act of creation, there was nothing. There wasn't empty space – there wasn't any space at all. God created space. God's act of creation did not occur at a particular time – before Creation there wasn't any time at all. God created time. Absolutely everything owes its existence to God: matter, energy, even space and time. After bringing everything into existence, Christians also believe that it was God who then formed and shaped everything to be the way we see it. But we believe that what God started off with was nothing at all, creation *ex nihilo*, creation from nothing. This understanding is also clear in the Bible passages in John 1:3, Colossians 1:16 and Revelation 4:11 quoted above.

Returning to Hebrews 11:3, the first half of the verse also tells us something very important. *By faith we understand that the universe was formed at God's command.* This point is vital. It is by means of faith that we understand that the universe was formed at God's command. Not by science: not by philosophy but by faith. Neither science nor philosophy will ever be able to prove conclusively whether God exists or not. Science and philosophy can only ever tell us about this universe of space and time. The God of the Bible is greater than the whole universe, beyond space and outside time. We know God is Creator in the same way that we know anything else about God, through believing what God has chosen to reveal of Himself to us.

However, when Christians say that we know God created the world because "the Bible says so" that is not going to be a convincing argument for other people even though Christians know it to be true. When we already have faith in God it is easy to see that God must exist and that God is the Creator of everything that exists. But when a person does not have faith in God already then it is not usually going to be possible to give them any kind of indisputable proof which will convince them that God exists or that God created the universe. What we believe about God as Creator follows on from other things we believe about God. We have already talked about the reasons Christians have for believing that God exists: who Jesus is and what Jesus did and above all about the historical fact that Jesus was crucified but on the third day he rose from the dead. We can point to our own experiences of God acting in our own lives and in the lives of people we know. Then when people have faith in Jesus they come to trust the Bible. And at that point we can explain how we know that God is Creator and how we know that we can trust what the Bible teaches. When somebody already believes in God then we can show them how God creating the universe is not contradicted by science or philosophy. In fact, both science and philosophy give us good reasons to believe that God exists and that God created everything. But those reasons will not usually be convincing proofs that God is the Creator if somebody doesn't already believe. It is *by faith we understand that the universe was formed at God's command.* I quote again J. B. Phillips. "God is not discoverable or demonstrable by purely scientific means, unfortunately for the scientifically-minded. But that really proves nothing. It simply means that the wrong instruments are being used for the job."

Science develops theories based on observations about the universe. Almighty God is by definition greater than the universe and outside and beyond and before the universe. So we need faith to recognise what God has chosen to reveal of Himself within the universe.

All Christians agree that God is Creator. Where Christians hold different opinions is over how God created the universe and particularly how long it all took. There are two major alternative understandings of this point.

"Young Earth Creationists" also called "7-Day Creationists"

This understanding reads the first two chapters of Genesis entirely literally. So "7-Day Creationists" believe that God made the universe from nothing in just six days of 24 hours each. From the ages of Adam and all his descendants they calculate that the earth was created only some thousands of years BC and so the earth is now less than 10,000 years old. This is why they are described as "Young Earth Creationists" or "7-Day Creationists". This view is most often associated with the doctrine of 'inerrancy', the idea that the Bible correctly records every detail of science and history "without error".

This understanding is sharply opposed to the view of scientists who think the universe is between 13 and 14 billion years old, that the earth is 4.5 billion years old and that human beings like us have been around for two hundred thousand years or so. Scientific theories such as evolution and the existence of dinosaurs in biology and continental drift in geology seem to contradict the idea of the entire creation taking only seven days.

"Old Earth Creationists"

There are very many other Christians who don't see the same problems with theories of evolution or dinosaurs or continental drift. "Old Earth Creationists" still believe just as strongly that the God of the Bible is Creator of the whole universe. But they disagree that everything came to be just as it is now in the space of just 144 hours only 6000 years ago. "Old Earth Creationists" believe that God created what scientists observe as "natural processes" like evolution or continental drift and then God worked through those processes to shape planet earth and all the life on it over billions of years. "Old Earth Creationists" are happy to accept that the theories of science describe how God made the earth while the Bible explains who made the earth and why. Variations of this understanding are labelled theistic evolution or evolutionary creationism.

"Young Earth Creationism" is very popular with American Christians. On the other hand, Christians in Britain, including most who would describe themselves as evangelicals, are more often "Old Earth Creationists." But which view is right? The truth is we just don't know. We won't be sure until we get to heaven. Different Christian friends and fellow Ministers hold strongly to both views. My own understanding has been shaped by some years of studying then teaching science and then more years of studying theology and Biblical interpretation and I want to explain why I am an "Old Earth Creationist".

In essence, the debate between 7-day "Young Earth Creationism" and "Old Earth Creationism" is not a matter of science but of Biblical Interpretation for Christians. The key question is this. What do the 'days' in Genesis refer to? The whole weight of "Young Earth Creationism" rests on interpreting that word 'day' in Genesis chapters 1 and 2 as literal periods of 24 hours. "Young Earth Creationists" argue that if a person does not believe in creation in seven days of 24 hours then they don't believe in the authority of the Bible. But it is not necessary to believe in a 7-day creation to believe in the infallibility of the Bible. Old Earth creationists (like me) are every bit as committed to the authority and reliability of the Bible as anybody else. We are actually disagreeing over the interpretation of just one word as it is used in just three passages of Scripture. Just what does the word 'day' mean in Genesis chapters 1 and 2?

In the Bible the events of creation were revealed, not observed. In the account of Creation in Genesis chapter 1 there were no humans around until the Sixth Day so the Genesis account certainly did not come from direct human observation. It was revealed in some way to the author of Genesis. All revelations have to be subject to interpretation and in the Bible revelations are more often symbolic than literal.

There are different kinds of language in the Bible: some is symbolic or metaphorical. When we approach any passage in the Bible we must try to work out what kind of language that passage is written in. Eternal and spiritual truths, things we can never fully understand or adequately describe, often cannot be expressed in literal language. Instead religious truth is often expressed in words which are being used symbolically or poetically, using similes and metaphors, sometimes bending language almost to breaking point. We make big mistakes if we try to understand literally language which is intended to be understood symbolically.

For example, think about when Jesus told his parables. Was the "Good Samaritan" a real living person? Did a genuine "Prodigal Son" ever leave his father? Were those parables recording history? Surely these were instead carefully constructed stories conveying powerful spiritual truths. The parables did not necessarily relate to historical events. We have to ask similar questions about the Creation Narratives in Genesis chapters 1 and 2. Are they intended to be "scientific truth" in Twenty-First Century terms? Is the language literal or is it instead symbolic or poetical language?

"Old Earth Creationists", like me, are just as committed as anybody else to the reliability of the Bible as the Word of God. But we believe that Genesis is teaching religious and not scientific truth. Therefore we believe that the language in the Biblical account of creation is metaphorical and symbolic rather than necessarily literal. Genesis teaches who it was who created the earth (God) and why, but Genesis is not a scientific textbook to tell us how it all took place.

In the Bible the word "day" does not always refer to a 24-hour period. In particular, some words in Psalm 90 and 2 Peter chapter 3 are significant. *But do not forget this one thing, dear friends: With the Lord a day is like a thousand years, and a thousand years are like a day.* (2 Peter 3:8 quoting Psalm 90:4) If the days in Genesis are symbolic days from God's perspective rather than from a human point of view, much of the apparent conflict between science and the Bible disappears.

Old Earth Creationists interpret the seven "days" in Genesis 1 as long periods of time. Other parts of the account are surely symbolic. When God said, "Let there be light", what language did God speak in? God "breathed" into Adam's nostrils but what does it mean to say God breathes? The limitations of human language suggest that when we are talking about things which God "says" and "does" that language surely has to be symbolic. So when it says 'days' it is surely reasonable and permissible to understand that these are God's days. It is not necessary, and in my view it is mistaken, to insist that the days in Genesis chapters 1 and 2 have to be understood as literal periods of 24 hours. Even the sun and the moon by which we measure human days did not come into existence until the third day.

Notice how well the order of creation in Genesis 1 and 2 actually fits with scientific ideas of evolution, ideas which did not come alone till thousands of years after Genesis was written. So Old Earth Creationists have no problem with the idea of development or evolution. In that understanding, there could well have been dinosaurs, living and dying out before humans were created in that very long period of the Fifth Day.

Genesis says that God created human beings in his own image. There are various different and complementary understandings of what the Bible means by "the image of God" in human beings. We can talk of the mental image: the capacity to think and reason and to use language to communicate sophisticated ideas, including science. There is the creative image: our ability to create things with our hands and also the whole aesthetic aspect of our humanity in glorious art and inspiring music. There is the moral image: the ability to differentiate between good and evil, right and wrong, truth and lies and falsehood. There is the social image of God in human beings who are designed to live in relationships with each other and supremely in relationship with God Himself. Then there is the spiritual image: the ability to worship and pray and exercise faith and to love. Human beings are all set apart from the animals because we embody the mental image, the creative image, the moral image, the social image and the spiritual image of God. Biologists and psychologists cannot explain where these aspects of our humanity arose from – evolution cannot explain them. To Christians these elements of personhood are indeed evidence for the existence of God. The Bible tells us that God breathed the breath of life into human beings and "Old Earth Creationists" understand this as a specific act of creation at the beginning of human history giving to particular animals those qualities of the image of God which make us distinctively human.

The forms of language used by science and history as we know them have only existed from the Eighteenth Century onwards. But Genesis 1-2 must surely have been revealed by God to those writers in ways that the people then could understand, not in the language of history and science which weren't going to be invented for thousands of years. The Bible accounts need to be read in the context of the kinds of literature which were around when they were written, not as if they were written today just for us. Here is a little story to explain that important point.

A man walks into a doctor's surgery.
"Doctor, Doctor," he said. "I keep on singing 'The Green Green Grass of Home' all the time."
The Doctor replied, "You've got 'Tom Jones syndrome'."
"Really?" the man asked, "Is that common?"
The Doctor's answer: "It's not unusual!" Boom Boom.

We know what kind of story that is by the formula, beginning, "Doctor, Doctor" and ending "Boom, Boom". It is a joke. The joke only is only humorous if we know certain key facts: Tom Jones is a famous singer and two of his greatest hits are "The Green Green Grass of Home" and "It's not unusual." To work as a joke, it is completely irrelevant whether an actual man ever did walk into a specific doctor's surgery or not. It is a funny story. The genre of joke does not demand historicity. There are obvious reasons why we would not expect to find that story in the Bible because elements of it would be outside the time period: it would be anachronistic. In the same way, it would be anachronistic to find in Genesis the kind of literalism, or scientific details or even historical language which we use today, especially when describing events which occurred before human beings were around. That would be a misunderstanding of the kind of language Genesis contains.

I believe that "Young Earth Creationists" are fighting the wrong war on the wrong battleground. There is no necessity to prove to the scientific community that the earth came into being in 6 days of 24 hours long less than 10,000 years ago. That is not a question of science but a question of Biblical interpretation and systematic theology. Focus on proving that Creation only took seven days distracts people from the more important task of pointing to God as Creator. Almighty God is Creator of Heaven and Earth. The debate between science and seven day "Young Earth Creationism" is a red herring from the vital Christian message we have to proclaim about God as Creator. Public arguments over Young Earth Creationism are likely to drive people away from God, not bring them to God.

So how did God create the world? In literally seven days of 24 hours each, as "Young Earth Creationists" believe? Or through natural processes which geology and evolutionary biology describe, as "Old Earth creationists believe"? We cannot know the answer to that question this side of heaven. What the Bible definitely teaches is that Almighty God is the Creator of Heaven and Earth. With the eye of faith, we can see the Hand of the Designer, the eternal Architect, in all He has made. And science which studies the wonders of creation will never ever be able to prove or disprove the existence of the Creator who is beyond and above His creation.

"You are worthy, our Lord and God, to receive glory and honour and power, for you created all things, and by your will they were created and have their being."
(Revelation 4:11)

Meeting God in Creation

For many people the question of whether or not God created the earth is not settled by intellectual debate, but rather when they encounter God in Creation for themselves. Some discover God in the beauty of a sunset or the night sky, others in the sheer scale and power of thunderstorms and waves crashing on to the shore. Many people are touched by the wonder of childbirth. I have encountered God many times in such ways.

It was just before four in the morning when the talking outside the tent became too much and I just had to crawl out to discover what was going on. The eastern sky was pale blue but the valley below was still in darkness. Then it happened! The next peak seemed to catch fire as the first rays of dawn struck the glacier and the snow and ice glowed deep red, then pink and orange. Of all the spectacles in the world, few can be as beautiful or as breath-taking as a sunrise over the Alps. That memory from almost 40 years ago always comes back whenever I am under canvas once again, or spend any time in the mountains. With it come these words from the Bible: *"The heavens declare the glory of God; the skies proclaim the work of his hands."* (Psalm 19:1)

One evening years later on a different camping holiday we all went up on a hilltop in pitch darkness, so far from towns that there was no glow of streetlights reflected in the sky. It took some minutes for our eyes to adjust to night vision. Only then did we discover that the ground was not completely dark. The chalk stones were luminous white, and for the first time I saw a field alive with the cold green fires of glow-worms. The clouds cleared and looking up I saw the panorama of the night sky. The stars appeared all the brighter because there was no moon. The sense of the vastness of the universe and the insignificance of man was overwhelming. And I recalled that the Bible describes God as *"the Father of the heavenly lights."* (James 1:17)

There, away from people and traffic, there were only the sounds of the insects and the night animals and the distant sea and the wind. And in the silence God could begin to speak. Such experiences of the beauties of nature may be common to country folk. But to town and city-dwellers they are rare and very precious. We are so used to surrounding ourselves with people and noise and the things man has made. We feel so much more secure when we are shielded from the elements in our safe warm dry homes in the middle of lots of other people and houses.

The science-fiction writer Isaac Asimov has painted a chilling picture of where this may end. He describes a future of vast underground cities, where the inhabitants of these 'Caves of Steel' are too terrified to go up to the surface. They simply cannot cope with the sight of the open air and the sky and the sun. People who live in large cities and especially in high-rise blocks may already understand such a sense of insulation from the natural world. But separated from nature, we may also be distanced from its Creator, Who is our Maker too. We can hide away from God in our man-made buildings and the bright lights of a busy town. It is much harder to ignore God when his glory shines through a spectacular sunset or the majestic star-filled sky or a glow-worm's beauty. Sometimes God seems hard to find. If that is so, we can try looking for Him in the world He has made.

"O Lord, our Lord, how majestic is your name in all the earth! When I consider your heavens, the work of your fingers, the moon and the stars which you have set in place, what is man that you are mindful of him, the son of man that you care for him?" (Psalm 8:1, 3-4)

8 Can we trust the New Testament?

Sometimes people who are not Christians will say, "You can't believe the New Testament." "It was all made up by the disciples." "Jesus never existed." As Christians, what can we say in response? We will think about the most important aspect of that question, the four Gospels written by Matthew, Mark, Luke and John. How can we be sure that what they tell us about Jesus is true?

What the Bible says about itself

Luke's Gospel begins with this introduction.
Many have undertaken to draw up an account of the things that have been fulfilled among us, just as they were handed down to us by those who from the first were eye-witnesses and servants of the word. Therefore, since I myself have carefully investigated everything from the beginning, it seemed good also to me to write an orderly account for you, most excellent Theophilus, so that you may know the certainty of the things you have been taught. (Luke 1:1-4)

The writer of Luke's Gospel tells us that after careful investigation he is recording for us the things Jesus said and did. He states that we can trust what we read because we have the testimony of eyewitnesses, the accounts *just as they were handed down to us by those who from the first were eye-witnesses and servants of the word.* These eyewitnesses were not only the apostles but also all the other Christians who had seen and heard Jesus and were reporting their own experiences. All these people were part of the Early Church and the Gospels written by Matthew, Mark, Luke and John were only accepted by the wider church because all these eyewitnesses confirmed that they were accurate accounts of Jesus's life and ministry as very many people remembered it. All this was written down *so that you may know the certainty of the things you have been taught.*

Luke, who wrote his gospel and also the book of Acts, was himself an eyewitness of the events in the Early Church which he records from the second half of Acts when he joined Paul on his missionary journeys. Luke says he *carefully investigated* all the other accounts he could lay his hands on to produce his own summary of the life and teaching of Jesus which we have as Luke's Gospel.

When it comes to John's Gospel, careful study has convinced me that traditions dating from the Early Church are true and that the author of the Fourth Gospel and of the three letters carrying his name was indeed the apostle John, one of Jesus's inner circle of Peter. James and John. There are many tell-tale signs in his Gospel that John was himself an eyewitness of the events he recorded. There is also a little section at the end of John's Gospel talking about its author which was clearly added by somebody else which acts as a testimonial to him. *This is the disciple who testifies to these things and who wrote them down. We know that his testimony is true.* (John 21:24)

So John himself had seen and heard Jesus. At the beginning of his first letter. John explicitly claims to have met and been with Jesus.
That which was from the beginning, which we have heard, which we have seen with our eyes, which we have looked at and our hands have touched – this we proclaim concerning the Word of life. The life appeared; we have seen it and testify to it, and we proclaim to you the eternal life, which was with the Father and has appeared to us. We proclaim to you what we have seen and heard, so that you also may have fellowship with us. And our fellowship is with the Father and with his Son, Jesus Christ.
(1 John 1:1-3)

The first Christians trusted John's report of what he had seen and heard and even touched and we can trust John too. I am similarly persuaded that the Gospel of Matthew was written by the apostle Matthew who witnessed the life and teaching of Jesus for himself. On the other hand, Mark's gospel was not written by an apostle, but probably by John Mark who was a companion of Paul and is mentioned in various letters written by Paul. Early church traditions written down by church leaders Papias, Irenaeus and Eusabius tell us that Mark faithfully wrote down the sermons of the apostle Peter. Peter passes on greetings from "my son Mark" at the end of his first letter. There are little bits of Mark's gospel which only Peter would have known about and people think that Mark himself is mentioned as the unnamed young man who was present when Jesus was arrested in the Garden of Gethsemane. If so, then Mark himself may well have been an eyewitness to the final days of Jesus's ministry.

The Gospels give us eyewitness accounts of the life of Jesus which are remarkably extensive and reliable historical documents. Some details we read about Jesus in the Gospels are confirmed for us by archaeology. Then outside of Christian sources, we can read about Jesus and the first Christians in Jewish and Roman writings. Before the end of the first century, the Jewish historian Josephus wrote this.

> "About this time there lived Jesus, a wise man, if indeed one ought to call him a man. For he was one who performed surprising deeds and was a teacher of such people as accept the truth gladly. He won over many Jews and many of the Greeks. He was the Christ. And when, upon the accusation of the principal men among us, Pilate had condemned him to a cross, those who had first come to love him did not cease. He appeared to them spending a third day restored to life, for the prophets of God had foretold these things and a thousand other marvels about him. And the tribe of the Christians, so called after him, has still to this day not disappeared".

Very soon after 100 AD, the Roman historian Tacitus refers in his Annals to the crucifixion of Jesus and the persecution of the Early Church by Emperor Nero. Around the same date the Roman Governor Pliny wrote a letter talking about the persecution of Christians. As evidence for events which happened 2000 years ago, these are all very good historical sources supporting the Gospel accounts.

The New Testament gives us the story of Jesus's life in the Four Gospels. The book of Acts, sometimes called The Acts of the Apostles, gives us a picture of the first Christians in the life of the Early Church. Then the letters attributed to the apostles Peter, James, John and Paul and other writers reveal a great deal about the things the Early Church believed and was teaching about Jesus. We can trust everything the New Testament teaches us about Jesus, because the churches in that time all agreed that the Four Gospels and Acts and also all of the letters were correct records and interpretations of the life and teaching of Jesus.

The Inspiration of the Bible

The second reason Christians have for trusting the Bible is that we believe the Holy Spirit inspired the writers. A letter written in the Early Church quite probably by the apostle Paul says this.

But as for you, continue in what you have learned and have become convinced of, because you know those from whom you learned it, and how from infancy you have known the holy Scriptures, which are able to make you wise for salvation through faith in Christ Jesus. All Scripture is God-breathed and is useful for teaching, rebuking, correcting and training in righteousness, so that the man of God may be thoroughly equipped for every good work. (2 Timothy 3:14-17)

All Scripture is *'God-breathed'.* That phrase does not imply that God dictated the words we read in the Bible to the individuals who wrote them down. What Christians understand by the idea of the inspiration of the Bible is that God the Holy Spirit was at work in the different writers in various ways so that what they wrote was precisely what God wanted to be written. Christians believe that the Bible is inspired by God. This is not saying that divine inspiration is the source of the Bible's authority for us. For example, Jesus said, *"I am the resurrection and the life. He who believes in me will live, even though he dies; and whoever lives and believes in me will never die."* (John 11:25-26) Those words have authority and power in our lives and bring us comfort and hope because of who Jesus is and because Jesus said them. The fact that the Gospel-writer was inspired when he wrote down his Gospel is secondary.

The authority comes from the Lord Jesus Christ who spoke those words. But the inspiration of Scripture is the guardian of that authority. We can trust that Jesus really did make all the wonderful promises we read in the Bible, because God inspired Matthew and Mark and Luke and John in their recording of what Jesus said. We can trust that Jesus really did do all the wonderful things we read about, because writers of the Gospels were inspired by the Holy Spirit. And we can trust that those authors and all the other New Testament writers had a correct understanding of who Jesus was and what he accomplished because all of them were inspired by the Holy Spirit to write exactly what God wants us to read.

So in the New Testament we have the testimony of eyewitnesses about Jesus and also the beliefs and understandings of the Early Church. These are guaranteed to be reliable for us as Christians by the work of the Holy Spirit who inspired the Bible. But somebody who is not a Christian could well say something like this. Saying we can trust the Bible just because it says it was written by eyewitnesses is circular reasoning. The writers claim they were eyewitnesses but perhaps they were lying. The Bible claims to be inspired by the Holy Spirit but that is not proof that it is. We have to be able to offer evidence from outside the Bible to convince us that it is true. And we find that proof in the countless experiences of God which all Christians and churches have had over the centuries.

The experiences of Christians

Churches and Christians through the centuries have recognised the books which we have as our Bible as a special kind of book which we call Holy Scripture. They have agreed that the Gospels are the testimony of eyewitness and that the letters sum up reliably for us the teaching of Jesus and the Apostles and of the Early Church. Churches and Christians have agreed that God has spoken to them through the Bible. They have agreed that they have met Jesus the Living Word through reading this Written Word. We have very good reasons to believe the Bible because of all the Churches and Christians before us who have believed the Bible.

Furthermore, Christians believe the Bible because we ourselves have met with Jesus as we have read and understood and believed it. Every occasion we have claimed a promise from Scripture and every occasion that God has answered our prayers is proof to us that the Bible is true and reliable. Every time God has helped us and comforted us and given us grace and peace and joy and love is proof that the Bible is true and reliable. Christians believe the Bible because again and again we have discovered for ourselves in our own experience that it is true.

The apostle John wrote, *"Jesus did many other miraculous signs in the presence of his disciples, which are not recorded in this book. But these are written that you may believe that Jesus is the Christ, the Son of God, and that by believing you may have life in his name."* (John 20:30-31) We trust the Bible because we ourselves have experienced that "life in all its fullness" which Jesus promises to give to everybody who follows Him. As Paul put it in 2 Timothy 3:15, the holy Scriptures have made us *"wise for salvation"*. In our own lives the Bible has been useful and effective *"for teaching, rebuking, correcting and training in righteousness, so that the man of God may be thoroughly equipped for every good work."* (2 Timothy 3:16-17). We have seen in other Christians and we know in our own lives the difference Jesus makes. But then there is also something else.

The inner witness of the Holy Spirit

We have the cumulative effects of all these experiences of God which convince us that the Bible is true. But, more than that, Christians also have God the Holy Spirit at work inside us telling us that we can trust the Bible. Theologians call this certainty "the inner witness of the Spirit." The Westminster Confession of faith was drawn up in the seventeenth century and generally agreed by all Protestant Christians. The Westminster Confession says this about the Bible.

> "We may be moved and induced by the testimony of the church to a high and revered esteem of the holy scripture, yet, notwithstanding, our full persuasion and assurance of the infallible truth, and divine authority thereof, is from the inward work of the Holy Spirit, bearing witness by and with the word in our hearts."

In modern language, we believe the Bible because the church through the ages has said it is true. But more than that, we also believe the Bible because of the inward work of the Holy Spirit in our own hearts assuring us that the Bible is true. The Holy Spirit inside us gives us a deep certainty that we can trust the Bible.

Everybody can experience this "inner witness of the Holy Spirit." J.B.Phillips wrote that the words of the New Testament "bear the hall-mark of reality and the ring of truth." Somebody once said, "Start reading the Bible as if it was like any other book and you will soon discover that it is unlike any other book." Read the Bible – free gift inside.

So we can certainly trust the New Testament. We believe it because it is the testimony of eyewitnesses and the teaching of the Early Church, guarded for us by the inspiration of the Holy Spirit. We believe the Bible because of the experiences of churches and of Christians through the centuries. We trust the Bible because God keeps speaking to us through what we read there even today. And we believe the Bible because of the "inner witness of the Holy Spirit" in our hearts.

The Gideons International place copies of the Bible in hotel rooms, hospitals and prisons, and give copies of the New Testament to young people entering secondary school every year. They provide the following introduction to the Bible.

"This Book is the mind of God, the state of man, the way of salvation, the doom of sinners, and the happiness of believers. Its doctrines are holy, its precepts are binding; its histories are true, and its decisions are immutable.

"Read it to be wise, believe it to be safe, practice it to be holy. It contains light to direct you, food to support you, and comfort to cheer you.

"It is the traveller's map, the pilgrim's staff, the pilot's compass, the soldier's sword, and the Christian's character. Here paradise is restored, heaven opened, and the gates of hell disclosed.

"Christ is its grand subject, our good its design, and the glory of God its end. It should fill the memory, rule the heart, and guide the feet. Read it slowly, frequently, prayerfully. It is a mine of wealth, a paradise of glory, and a river of pleasure."

Christians believe the Bible is God's Word for humanity. We should read it and study it and commit it to memory and let it shape our lives. *"These things are written that you may believe that Jesus is the Christ, the Son of God, and that by believing you may have life in his name."* (John 20:31)

9 Is Jesus the only way to God?

England is no longer a Christian country. Whether England ever was a Christian country where everybody went to church and everybody lived by the Ten Commandments is debatable. But it is certainly true that England is no longer a Christian Country. Christendom, where everybody shared common Christian beliefs and values, is rapidly being replaced by a multicultural, multi-faith society where Christianity is only one option amongst many.

We live in a consumer culture, where people expect the right to choose and satisfaction guaranteed every time. These expectations extend beyond shopping to morality, to relationships and even to religion. So some people who take an interest in spiritual things shop around between the different religions until they find one that suits them. Other people like to pick-and-mix bits from different religions, a taste of Christian morality mixed with bits of Eastern mysticism, extracts from the Bible and quotations from the Koran, a sort of smorgasbord "eat whatever you like" buffet of religions. And, of course, with so many varieties of religion on offer, very many people can't be bothered to search for the truth and so they choose not to choose at all. "I don't buy into any of that stuff."

In this supermarket of beliefs, people object if somebody claims to have the one and only truth. In a world governed by political correctness it is considered impolite and offensive, or even in some circumstances against the law, to claim that you are right and everybody else is wrong. Yet in this politically correct but morally and spiritually bankrupt world Christians are obliged to stand up and be counted. Because we are convinced that Jesus is Lord. Not just "one Lord among many". Not just "Lord if you choose him to be your Lord". But Jesus is Lord. The Lord. The One and only Son of God. The one and only Saviour.

If people ask us why they should accept that Jesus Christ is Lord, or that Jesus is the only way to God, Christians need to be able to give an adequate answer. We need to be able to defend our faith, and explain why we are convinced that Jesus is unique. Here are five ways in which Jesus Christ stands apart from all other religious leaders.

Jesus's birth

The Bible tells us that Jesus was different from any other human being who has ever lived. Because Jesus was much more than a man. He was truly God, born as a human being. *"The virgin will be with child and will give birth to a son, and they will call him Immanuel"– which means, "God with us."* (Matthew 1:23)

Jesus Christ was not just another holy man: not just one more prophet among many. Jesus was God the Son.

In the beginning was the Word, and the Word was with God, and the Word was God. He was with God in the beginning. Through him all things were made; without him nothing was made that has been made. …

The Word became flesh and made his dwelling among us. We have seen his glory, the glory of the One and Only, who came from the Father, full of grace and truth.
(John 1:1-3, 14)

In this world with so many different religious leaders offering ways to find God, Christians believe that Jesus Christ is unique because he is indeed God, revealing Himself to us.

Jesus's teaching

The comedian Billy Connolly once said, "I don't believe in Christianity but I think Jesus was a wonderful man." Very many people who would not call themselves Christians still recognise that Jesus was the greatest moral teacher who ever lived. Many people claim to try to live their lives according to Jesus's teaching in the Sermon on the Mount. The teaching of Jesus Christ has shaped two thousand years of Western civilisation. Think about the stories Jesus told – the parables: the extraordinary forgiveness of the father who welcomes home the rebellious prodigal son; the Good Samaritan who unexpectedly helps a stranger in distress. And so many of Jesus's sayings have become part of everyday speech: the exhortations to "love your neighbour as yourself"; "love your enemies"; "turn the other cheek" and "go the extra mile".

Then look at some of the amazing claims Jesus made about Himself.
"I am the good shepherd. The good shepherd lays down his life for the sheep."
(John 10:11)

Jesus was a Jew and He was speaking to Jews, who all knew Psalm 23. There is only one shepherd of Israel. "The Lord is my shepherd." In saying to them, "I am the good shepherd", the implication of that was very clear. Jesus was saying, "I am your God!" Jesus also said many other astonishing things. *"I am the bread of life."* (John 6:35). *"I am the light of the world."* (John 8:12) *"I am the resurrection and the life."* (John 11:25) *"I am the way and the truth and the life."* (John 14:6) *"I am the true vine, and my Father is the gardener."* (John 15:1) Perhaps the most important claim Jesus made about Himself is found in John 10:30. *"I and the Father are one."* Not, "I am teaching you about God," but "I am God." Jesus's teaching was unique.

Jesus's ministry

Jesus's ministry was unique in history. The proof that everything Jesus claimed about himself is true is found in every one of his actions. Everything Jesus did revealed God's love. He forgave people's sins, like that woman caught in the very act of adultery. *"Neither do I condemn you. Go and sin no more."* (John 8:11) Jesus preached with a unique authority, not like other Jewish teachers who just quoted each other. Jesus preached on his own authority. *"Truly, truly, I tell you."* And then Jesus demonstrated that authority by driving out evil spirits. Jesus calmed the storm – even the wind and the waves obeyed Him. He walked on the water and fed the 5000 with just five loaves and two fishes. Jesus healed the sick, set people free from evil spirits and even raised the dead back to life. Jesus's miracles were God's love in action: concrete expressions of the Good News. All these things showing us the uniqueness of Jesus are illustrated in his response to a message sent by John the Baptist.

When the men came to Jesus, they said, "John the Baptist sent us to you to ask, 'Are you the one who was to come, or should we expect someone else?'"

At that very time Jesus cured many who had diseases, sicknesses and evil spirits, and gave sight to many who were blind. So he replied to the messengers, "Go back and report to John what you have seen and heard: The blind receive sight, the lame walk, those who have leprosy are cured, the deaf hear, the dead are raised, and the good news is preached to the poor. Blessed is the man who does not fall away on account of me."

(Luke 7:20-23)

If people ask what is so special about Jesus, we can encourage them to read the gospels, to read about His ministry. They will see for themselves that Jesus is unique. Napoleon Bonaparte once said this about Jesus.

> "I know men; and I tell you that Jesus Christ is not a man. Superficial minds see a resemblance between Christ and the founders of empires, and the gods of other religions. That resemblance does not exist. There is between Christianity and whatever other religions the distance of infinity.... Everything in Christ astonishes me. His spirit overawes me, and His will confounds me. Between him and whoever else in the world, there is no possible term of comparison. He is truly a being by Himself. His ideas and sentiments, the truth which he announces, His manner of convincing, are not explained either by human organization or by the nature of things.... The nearer I approach, the more carefully I examine, everything is above me — everything remains grand, of a grandeur which overpowers. His religion is a revelation from an intelligence which certainly is not that of man.... One can absolutely find nowhere, but in Him alone, the imitation or the example of His life.... I search in vain in history to find the similar to Jesus Christ, or anything which can approach the gospel. Neither history, nor humanity, nor the ages, nor nature, offer me anything with which I am able to compare it or to explain it. Here everything is extraordinary."[2]

Napoleon certainly recognised the uniqueness of Christ.

Jesus's death

All great religious leaders have died. The death of Jesus is different from the deaths of every other human being because his death itself had a significance which places it at the heart of the Christian faith. Jesus's death was not a tragic regrettable accident. Jesus Himself understood His death to be the lynchpin of God's plan of salvation!
"For even the Son of Man did not come to be served, but to serve, and to give his life as a ransom for many." (Mark 10:45)

The Early Church also recognised the importance of Jesus's death. The apostle Peter quotes Isaiah chapter 53 and writes *"He committed no sin, and no deceit was found in his mouth."* Peter continues, *Christ Himself carried our sins in his body to the cross so that we might die to sin and live for righteousness.*
(1 Peter 2:22 and 24)

---

[2] Cited by Vernon C. Grounds in *The Reason for Our Hope.*

Every great religious leader died as a consequence of their own sins. But the Bible tells us Jesus was completely innocent – without sin. Different from every other person, Jesus died for our sins, in our place. By paying the penalty for our sin on the cross, Jesus made a way for our sins to be forgiven. Jesus's death made the way for God to welcome us back as his beloved children. On the cross Jesus's last words were, *"It is finished!"* (John 19:30) This was not a cry of despair but of triumph. It is accomplished – the price is paid!

Somebody has explained the great difference between the Christian religion and every other religion in the world like this. Every other religion can be summed up in just two letters but the Christian faith needs four. Every other religion says "DO." Do this, do that, do the other and you will find salvation. But Christianity says, "It is DONE, it is accomplished, it is finished!" So the death of Jesus is unique – it is the only way to salvation, the only hope for human beings to escape the judgment of a holy God.

Jesus's resurrection

Here is the heart of the Good News of Jesus Christ and the supreme difference between Jesus and every other human being who has ever lived. All great religious leaders have died. But Jesus is different from everybody else. Jesus is didn't stay dead! Mohammed – dead and buried. Buddha – dead and buried. Every other founder of religions large and small – dead and buried. Jesus Christ – risen from the dead, never more to die! We thought about this in chapter 5. Didn't he used to be dead?

The apostle Paul recorded this early statement of Christian belief.
For what I received I passed on to you as of first importance: that Christ died for our sins according to the Scriptures, that he was buried, that he was raised on the third day according to the Scriptures, and that he appeared to Peter, and then to the Twelve. After that, he appeared to more than five hundred of the brothers at the same time, most of whom are still living, though some have fallen asleep. Then he appeared to James, then to all the apostles, and last of all he appeared to me also.
(1 Corinthians 15:3-8)

On the day of Pentecost, this was the heart of the apostle Peter's sermon. *"God has raised this Jesus to life, and we are all witnesses of the fact. Exalted to the right hand of God, he has received from the Father the promised Holy Spirit and has poured out what you now see and hear. ….. Therefore let all Israel be assured of this: God has made this Jesus, whom you crucified, both Lord and Christ."*
(Acts 2:32-33, 36)

The apostles were witnesses to the resurrection of Jesus Christ. This was the gospel they preached – Jesus is alive! The arrival of the Holy Spirit at Pentecost and the visible work of the Holy Spirit in the world through history and still today are God's proof that Jesus is risen from the dead and that Jesus is Lord. The difference Jesus makes in the lives of Christians is proof that Jesus is still alive today.

So Jesus Christ is unique. Jesus is not just better than all the founders of other religions. In who he was and the things he did, Jesus stands out apart from them in every way. His birth was unique. His teaching was unique. His ministry was unique. His death was unique. His resurrection was unique. And this is what Jesus said about himself. *"I am the way and the truth and the life. No-one comes to the Father except through me.* (John 14:6)

We live in a world which has lost its way. A world which says that all ways lead to God: "you pays your money and you takes your choice." But Jesus Christ says, *"I am the way"*, the Way, the one and only way. *"No-one comes to the Father except through me."* We live in a world which has abandoned the idea of absolute truth. People say, "We each have our own truth, it's all relative and one person's truth is as good as any other." But Jesus Christ says, *"I am the truth"*, the Truth, the one and only ultimate truth! *"No-one comes to the Father except through me."* We live in a world where people are looking for the meaning of life in all the wrong places. And Jesus Christ says, *"I am the life"*, the Life, the one and only way to find life in all its fullness. *"No-one comes to the Father except through me."*

Jesus is the only way to God. This is what the first Christians believed and this is what they preached. "*Salvation is found in no one else, for there is no other name under heaven given to men by which we must be saved."* (Acts 4:12) Jesus is the only way to God. This is the message entrusted to the church. This is the message to which the Holy Spirit is the Witness. Jesus Christ is the only way and truth and life. Jesus who was more than a man – who was the God born as a human being, the truth of God incarnate. Jesus who revealed God through His teaching and through His Holy character. Jesus who healed the sick and raised the dead. Jesus who died on the cross as a ransom for many. Jesus who was dead but now is risen from the dead and now lives forever. It is this Jesus Christ who declares to people of every faith and no faith, *"No-one comes to the Father except through me."*

10 How can we believe in God in a world so full of suffering?

Where was God in Paris on the evening of Friday the 13 of November 2015? That was the evening teams of Islamic State terrorists launched three separate attacks in Paris with machine guns and bombs. 129 people were murdered and more than 350 others were injured. In the following weeks people were asking important questions. "Why doesn't God do something to stop terrorists before they kill innocent people?" "Doesn't the presence of so much evil in the world prove that God doesn't exist at all?" "How can we believe in God in a world so full of suffering?" Just where was God in Paris on that Friday evening?

When we think about human suffering, all kinds of examples come to mind. The plight of refugees fleeing the evils of Islamic State. Famines and floods. The millions starving without food and the billions surviving without safe drinking water or the basics of medical care. All the individuals killed or maimed in car crashes and house fires. Sometimes people we know who are in agony from terrible diseases. And we may be experiencing suffering and grief in different situations ourselves. How can we believe in God in a world so full of suffering? This is one of the six big questions which people who are not Christians want an answer to. As Christians we need to be prepared to give an answer which is true and satisfying. The question was asked after the horrors of Auschwitz and Belsen. It came to a focus in Britain after the massacres at Locherbie and Dunblane and throughout the world after the destruction of the Twin Towers of the World Trade Centre. Where was God in those places when so many innocent people were suffering and dying?

In many events, responsibility for the suffering obviously rests with people and with deliberate acts of evil. In some other situations, nobody is to blame and nobody should be blamed. "Natural disasters" and tragic accidents happen and they could have happened to any one of us. So the question is very straightforward: why does God allow such accidents to happen? The problem of what is called "innocent suffering" is a vital issue for Christians to grapple with. It is a question which people who are not Christians will sometimes offer as their proof that God doesn't exist at all. "If there was a God then he wouldn't allow that kind of suffering," they say. To some people the very existence of innocent suffering is a knockdown argument which demonstrates to them that there cannot be a God at all.

The classic formulation of the problem of innocent suffering goes something like this.
If God is all-powerful, he COULD stop all suffering.
If God is all-loving, He WOULD stop all suffering.
So does the presence of suffering in the world prove that God is NOT all-loving?
Or does it prove that God is NOT all-powerful?
Or does it prove that God doesn't exist at all?

In reality, when you stop to think about it, that argument doesn't tell us anything about God's existence at all. "If there was a God, he wouldn't allow innocent people to suffer," people say. But saying, "if there was a God" in that kind of way is actually already making some important assumptions about the nature of God. It assumes at least that God exists, that God is good, that God is just, that God is loving. Unless God exists, and unless God is good and just and loving, there is no reason to expect the world to be any different from the way it is. Unless God exists and is good and just and loving, there would be no reason to expect him to do anything to stop innocent suffering. At the same time the question also assumes that a God exists who is powerful enough to change events in the world if he wanted to. A God who was not all-powerful could not be expected to do anything about innocent suffering.

So the person who asks, "where is God when innocent people are suffering?" is already assuming that a God exists who is not only good and just and loving but who is also powerful enough to prevent innocent suffering if He so chooses. The question is not really about whether God exists at all, but rather about the character of God: whether he is really the kind of God we believe him to be, in the light of events in the world which suggest the opposite. The heart of the problem of innocent suffering is really best expressed like this. "Why does a good and just and loving and all-powerful God not intervene to prevent innocent people from suffering?" Does this mean that God is not really good and just and loving? Or does it mean that God isn't really all-powerful after all?

In response to this question Christians want to say a number of things.

God IS good and just

The Bible teaches us in so many places that God is perfect in His justice, goodness, righteousness and fairness. The Bible talks about righteousness more than 500 times and justice almost 200. We are only human, limited in our wisdom and understanding. The Bible assures us that God rules the world with complete justice and fairness. And as well as being a good and just God, the Bible makes clear that God is Almighty.

God IS all-powerful

The God of the Bible is God ALMIGHTY, Maker of heaven and earth and all that is in them. We see God's mighty power at work in the work of Creation, in the events of the Exodus and in the miracles of Jesus. So, since God is both good and just, and also all-powerful, why does God not intervene to bring innocent suffering to an end? The best answer to that question lies in the reality of the free will of human beings to make choices.

Suffering is an inevitable consequence of human free will

So much suffering of innocent people is actually caused directly or indirectly by the sinful actions of human beings. This is obvious in murder and war and acts of terrorism, where the powerful inflict terrible suffering on the powerless. Equally, very many of the world's problems are caused by human greed. There is enough food to go round. So often, it just doesn't get to the people who are starving at prices they can afford to pay. And there is enough land for people to be able to build homes in safety, instead of on flood plains or along fault lines or in the shadows of volcanoes.

At the same time, life for everybody is full of risks. Where we live. What we eat. How we travel. All these decisions carry risks of us being harmed in some way. Sometimes circumstances lead to totally unanticipated accidents which could happen to anybody. But more often, somewhere along the way, human beings have made some choices which have made the accident a possibility. We have decided to put ourselves into a position where there is a risk, however small, that we might be hurt. Or other people have done something which unintentionally and unforeseeably sets in motion the chain of events which leads to somebody somewhere suffering. The only way God could prevent those kinds of accidents would be to prevent everybody from ever taking any risks.

The only sure-fire way that God could deal with the problem of innocent suffering would be to make sure that nobody could ever harm anybody else. But the only way to do that would be to get rid of all the people who could ever possibly, conceivably cause harm to others maybe, one day, not just by deliberate action but by omission or even by accident. And that would mean all of us, everybody, the whole human race. Because we are all human, all fallen, all sinful. We all have free will. Any one of us could choose to hurt another. We all make bad choices. And we are all fallible, all imperfect. Any one of us by our mistakes and failures and accidents could cause others to suffer, even if that was the last thing we intended. So the only way God could get rid of innocent suffering completely would be to get rid of all the people. God could do this: God is Almighty. But at the same time, God is also all-loving.

God IS loving and merciful

The God of the Bible is the God of love and of mercy. The Bible tells us, "God is love." The reason that God doesn't solve the problem of innocent suffering by the simple plan of wiping out all the people is obvious proof of God's love and mercy. On the other hand, if God were to intervene in miraculous ways to prevent every incident of innocent suffering, what a strange world we would live in. The car with brakes failing wouldn't hit the pedestrian, because God would lift the pedestrian ten feet into the air as the car crashed beneath him. The African village wouldn't be swept away because, just as in the parting of the Red Sea, the floodwaters would separate and flow each side of the village instead of through it. The starving millions might discover that stones really do turn to bread for them each day. That would indeed be a world full of strange miracles. It would be a very confusing unpredictable world to live in. But that is not the world which God has created.

Christians believe in a God of miracles. We believe in a God who does act in power to bring healing and deliverance and salvation. But we also recognise that God only works in those kinds of ways in rare and exceptional circumstances, nowadays usually in His church and for His praise and glory and not usually in the wider world which does not even believe He exists. God alone has the wisdom and justice to decide fairly when it is right for Him to intervene by miracles and when to let events run their natural course, however tragic the outcome. We need to trust in God's justice and fairness. And we recognise that it is actually a sign of God's love and mercy that, although He is all-powerful, God generally does allow the world to continue in its own way, with natural laws operating unhindered and events unfolding in predictable ways. For most of the time, God leaves human beings to take responsibility for our lives, and to take care of each other as best we are able. Because the only alternative would be to bring this world to an end and make a radically different new world!

Somebody once asked the German preacher and theologian Helmut Thielicke what he thought was the most important question facing the Western World. He pointed to the question of suffering.

> "Again and again I have the feeling that suffering is regarded as something which is fundamentally inadmissible, distressing, embarrassing, and not to be endured. Naturally, we are called upon to combat and diminish suffering. All medical and social action is motivated by the perfectly justified passion for this goal. But the idea that suffering is a burden which <u>can or even should</u> be fundamentally radically exterminated can only lead to disastrous illusions. One perhaps does not even have to be a Christian to know that suffering belongs to the very nature of this our world and will not pass away until this world passes away. And beyond this, we Christians know that in a hidden way it is connected with man's reaching for the forbidden fruit, but that God can transform even this burden of a fallen world into a blessing and fill it with meaning."

"Suffering is part of the very nature of this our world," said Thielicke. It would be a very, very different world which did not have such suffering. The continued existence of evil and the possibility of innocent suffering are both consequences of God's mercy and patience. He could just bring judgement on us all here and now and that would be and end of it! Until that judgement comes, there will always be suffering.

It is interesting that this issue of innocent suffering is generally only seen to be a challenge to faith in God in the Developed World where life has become generally comfortable for most people for most of the time. In parts of the Developing World, in Africa and India and South America, suffering and death are much more a part of the circle of everyday life. In these places people recognise the reality of our human condition – there will always be suffering. And yet there many more people put their trust in God.

The fact is that human beings do have free will. And in the world as it is, the only way God could remove the evil and suffering from the world would be to take away all human freedom of choice. Somebody may ask, "Why doesn't God do something to stop terrorists before they kill innocent people?" The answer is simple. Because the only way God could stop evil people from doing evil things would be to take away freedom of choice from all of us, for all of the time! God chooses not to do that. God chooses to give human beings free will and leave us all with free will. We are able to make choices and sometimes we make bad choices.

But, some people may object, if God knew that human choice would lead to so much evil and suffering why did He give us free will in the first place? There are a number of different Christian answers to that question and here are three of them.

(a) Our experiences of suffering and evil are in some ways "good for us". They teach us to make good choices, develop character, inspire faith and so "refine our souls". See Romans 5:3-5. This view goes all the way back to the Second Century bishop Irenaeus.

(b) God wants us to love him freely, not because we are programmed to do so like robots. Human free will and the resulting evil and suffering are necessary so that we have a genuine free choice either to love or to reject God. The world is "a Vale of Soul-Making"; a phrase attributed to the Twentieth Century philosopher John Hick.

(c) The existence of so much evil and suffering in the world are necessary so that God's divine and mysterious purposes can be fulfilled. As limited human beings, we may never understand God's plan in this life but in heaven we will understand why so much evil and suffering was allowed. In various ways suffering can bring benefits, for example it refines faith (1 Peter 1:3-9) and develops perseverance, character and hope (Romans 5:1-5). And there will also be other consequences of suffering so profound that we will never be able to fathom them.

God is good and just, God is all-powerful and God is loving and merciful. In His wisdom he leaves the world to carry on and doesn't prevent innocent suffering by continually intervening. But we mustn't conclude that God is aloof or unaffected when people are suffering and dying. Because last, but by no means least, there is something else very important which Christians want to say.

God shares our sufferings

Sometimes even Christians can feel that God doesn't know what is going on in his world, or that He doesn't care about us anymore. But Almighty God became a human being in Jesus Christ. And when we reflect on the events of the last week of his earthly ministry we are reminded why Jesus the Saviour has been the strength and inspiration for so many people who have suffered. Through the ages, the poor and the oppressed and the slaves, the sick and the suffering and the dying, have found comfort and hope not only in the resurrection of Jesus, but also in His dying on the cross for them. Because more than anywhere else, it was on the cross that Jesus the Son of God became one with all human beings and took upon himself our pains and our sufferings

After the massacre at Dunblane in 1996, Steve Chalke wrote some wise words which apply to so many situations of innocent suffering.

> "We know that what happened was neither His doing nor His will. God's was the first heart to break over the events that took place there. He wept with us for the children whose lives were cut short and the family they left behind. When confronted with the pain of the death of his friend Lazarus, Jesus also wept."

God is still suffering right now alongside each and every one of millions of people who are injured and dying and bereaved and homeless and terrified. God suffers with the communities shattered by every dreadful tragedy. God suffers with the thousands dying in floods and famines and conflicts, and with the tens of thousands dying of hunger and of terrible diseases every day. We never know about their innocent suffering but God sees it all in intimate detail. God suffered with the bereaved and the injured in Paris in November 2015. And God suffers just as much with the all victims of war and terrorism everywhere.

God suffers with us in every incident of innocent suffering, and God knows the agony of that suffering so well because there was none so innocent as Jesus, the Son of God, the spotless Lamb of God who took away the sins of the world. There, dying on the cross, Jesus experienced grief and pain as deep as any human being before or since. God suffers with us. So, how can we believe in God in a world so full of suffering? Because we know that, wherever people are suffering, God is also there suffering with us. Where was God in Paris on that Friday evening in 2015? God was there, weeping with the rest of us.

11 What happens when we die?

Here is a very important question. It is a question many people spend a lot of time thinking about and many other people try hard to avoid thinking about. What happens when we die? Three score years, and then – what?

The only way we can really know the answer to that question would be if somebody came back from the dead to tell us. So the only person in history we can trust for the answer is Jesus Christ. Jesus Christ is the Son of God. Jesus died on the cross but three days later God raised Him from the dead. And Jesus has revealed to us the truth about life after death, the glorious hope of heaven which Christians share and which everybody can discover for themselves in the Bible. We will consider what the Bible teaches about life after death and then we will need to think about some wrong ideas which some people have, which are as confusing and dangerous as they are mistaken.

Death is the ultimate statistic – one out of one die. Some people see no hope beyond death. Bertrand Russell wrote, "There is no splendour, no vastness anywhere. Only triviality for a moment, and then nothing." In contrast, Christians are guaranteed not a hopeless end, but an endless hope. The Bible tells us about what happens when we die. As Christians we have been saved – our sins have been forgiven, we have been born again to eternal life. We are being saved – we enjoy that life in all its fullness which comes from our relationship with God as our heavenly Father. But the best is yet to come. We will be saved. One day Christ will transform our lowly bodies so they will become like His heavenly body. Now we see as in a glass darkly, then we will see face to face. Now we know in part, then we shall know even as we ourselves are known. This is our wonderful Christian hope.

But our citizenship is in heaven. And we eagerly await a Saviour from there, the Lord Jesus Christ, who, by the power that enables him to bring everything under his control, will transform our lowly bodies so that they will be like his glorious body.
(Philippians 3:20-21)

Martin Lloyd-Jones wrote,

> "We have a new citizenship, we are in Christ, and because we are in Christ, we are seated in the heavenly places with him. Certain things will happen to us before we finally arrive in heaven, but our citizenship is as definite now as it will be then. There will be a physical translation when we die, but spiritually we are there already, we belong there."

The apostle Paul talked about this wonderful hope we have as Christians.
What you sow does not come to life unless it dies. When you sow, you do not plant the body that will be, but just a seed, perhaps of wheat or of something else. But God gives it a body as he has determined, and to each kind of seed he gives its own body. …
So will it be with the resurrection of the dead. The body that is sown is perishable, it is raised imperishable; it is sown in dishonour, it is raised in glory; it is sown in weakness, it is raised in power; it is sown a natural body, it is raised a spiritual body. If there is a natural body, there is also a spiritual body.
(1 Corinthians 15:36-38, 42-44)

So God has promised to give us a new kind of body which will be appropriate for heaven. Heaven will be so different and so wonderful that our human minds cannot even imagine it, but the Bible does give us different pictures of heaven. It will be like a city, a place of community. It will be like a party, a celebration. It will be a place of continual glorious worship. Most of all we will be in the very presence of God. Jim Packer wrote, "We know very little about heaven, but a theologian once described it as 'an unknown region with a well-known inhabitant.'"

To believers who have learned to love and trust Jesus, the prospect of meeting him face to face and being with him forever is the hope that keeps us going, no matter what life may throw at us. The Puritan pastor Richard Baxter expressed our Christian hope like this.

> My knowledge of that life is small, The eye of faith is dim,
> But it's enough that Christ knows all, And I shall be with him.

One question which Christians sometimes ask is this. Do believers go straight to heaven when they die? Or must we wait for the resurrection of the dead when Christ returns? We need to remember that what we call life 'after' death is not simply some chronological continuation of this life. Heaven is life in the presence of God and in His eternal Kingdom.

Like God Himself, 'eternal' life is not only everlasting but also more importantly outside all time as we know it. From the perspective of people who are still alive, it might appear that the body of a dead person is 'asleep' and awaiting Christ's Return. But Jesus promised the repentant thief hanging on the next cross, *"Today you will be with me in Paradise"* (Luke 23:53). So we can be sure that believers enter the presence of Christ immediately when we die. We will not be waiting around in some kind of 'limbo'. Christians who have died are already with Christ in glory.

This is what the Bible teaches about life after death. This is the Christian hope. But at the same time there are some wrong ideas around about what happens when we die. They are popular ideas but they are sadly mistaken. The first mistaken idea is that people in this life can make contact with those who have died. People try all kinds of ways to do this. Some turn to mediums and séances and spiritualism or spiritism. Others look to Ouija boards or other 'mechanical' ways to reach beyond the grave. Some people are motivated by deep grief to try to stay in touch with loved ones who have died. Others are driven by fear of their own death, or fear of the future, or simply by curiosity. Whatever the motives, attempts to make contact with dead people are tragic, futile and potentially very dangerous.

A friend of mine, Ben Alexander was once one of Britain's leading spiritualist mediums. Then he became a Christian and since then Ben has spent his life warning people of the great dangers of spiritualism, séances, mediums, Ouija boards, clairvoyance and all other attempts to contact the dead. Ben's book, *Out of Darkness,* is full of examples of truly dreadful things that have happened to people who have dabbled in spiritualism and similar doorways to danger. People cannot contact the dead – they only come into contact with forces of evil. For that reason, all attempts to communicate with the dead are explicitly forbidden and condemned by God in the Bible.

When you enter the land the LORD your God is giving you, do not learn to imitate the detestable ways of the nations there. Let no-one be found among you who sacrifices his son or daughter in the fire, who practises divination or sorcery, interprets omens, engages in witchcraft, or casts spells, or who is a medium or spiritist or who consults the dead. Anyone who does these things is detestable to the LORD, and because of these detestable practices the LORD your God will drive out those nations before you.
(Deuteronomy 18:9-12)

Attempting to contact the dead carried the death penalty in Israel, and cost King Saul his life. All attempts involve a real danger of contact with the forces of evil. Anyone who has dabbled in spiritualism or any such form of the occult is strongly advised to seek the help of a Christian Minister. Spiritualism, mediums and séances are cruel lies and only deceive people with false hopes.

But what about "them up there"? Are our late lamented loved ones looking down on us cheering us on? Does the communion of the saints mean that the saints in heaven can see and hear us and occasionally slip us words of encouragement and comfort? Some people understand Hebrews 12:1 in that way. *Therefore, since we are surrounded by such a great cloud of witnesses, let us throw off everything that hinders and the sin that so easily entangles, and let us run with perseverance the race marked out for us.*

We need to understand that the word 'witnesses' here does not mean that people who have died are watching us from on high witnessing how we live our lives. Instead it refers to those believers throughout history whose lives of faith are a witness to us of God's faithfulness. The Bible tells us that contact between this world and heaven is impossible. Jesus made this very clear in His parable of the Rich Man and Lazarus.
"But Abraham replied, 'Son, remember that in your lifetime you received your good things, while Lazarus received bad things, but now he is comforted here and you are in agony. And besides all this, between us and you a great chasm has been fixed, so that those who want to go from here to you cannot, nor can anyone cross over from there to us.'" (Luke 16:25-26)

There can be no contact between this world and the next, in either direction. That is the way God has said it should be. And God knows best.

There is another very popular but equally mistaken idea about life after death. It concerns 'ghosts' and other expressions of what is termed 'the paranormal'. The idea is that when some people die, instead of "passing over to the other side" or on to the afterlife, they get trapped in this world and appear as 'ghosts'. The idea is very popular in films and television programmes, from Casper the Friendly Ghost and Ghostbusters to the comedy Randall and Hopkirk Deceased, about a private detective who was aided and abetted by his former partner who was a ghost. To emphasise, these stories are fiction.

In the Bruce Willis film "The Sixth Sense", endlessly repeated on television, an eight-year-old boy called Cole has terrifying experiences. "I see dead people," he says. "Walking around like regular people. They don't see each other. They only see what they want to see. They don't know they're dead." "(I see them) all the time. They're everywhere." The same plot device is at the heart of the film "Ghost", with Patrick Swayze haunting Demi Moore. In that story, fake psychic Oda Mae Brown played by Whoopi Goldberg explains things like this. "He's stuck, that's what it is. He's in between worlds. You know it happens sometimes that the spirit gets yanked out so fast that the essence still feels it has work to do here." Popular entertainment spreads this idea that when some people die they don't go to heaven but they stick around on earth haunting people as 'ghosts' or 'restless spirits', especially if they have some unfinished business left on earth or if they really, really loved somebody. Again, these stories are pure fiction.

Many people waste their time and money looking for ghosts and chasing what are called paranormal experiences. Some go to psychics; others turn to different forms of fortune telling or magic. Again the Bible make clear that this search is both pointless and potentially very dangerous. Ghosts do not exist.

Many people certainly have some very odd experiences. A number of people I know and trust have told me about very strange things they have seen and heard and felt. Those experiences can be psychological but they can also be encounters with the supernatural. The fatal mistake is to think that these ghosts and poltergeists and apparitions have anything to do with people who have died. When people do have these kinds of experiences of the supernatural, the Bible is clear that it is not the ghosts of dead people they meet. Instead it is those very real supernatural beings which the Bible calls evil spirits or demons. Over the years our churches have helped a number of folk whose lives had been damaged by encounters with demons, sometimes leaving them in desperate situations. The power of the name of Jesus Christ can set anyone free.

But the warnings in the Bible are very clear. Living people cannot communicate with dead people and we should never try. And there are no such things as the ghosts of dead people wandering restlessly among the living. There is only the reality of evil spirits, also called demons, seeking to distract people away from God.

On the other hand, as Christians we have the wonderful hope of eternal life, life in all its fullness here and now which not even death can take away. This Christian hope is not some vague optimism but a happy certainty. Hope is a combination of expectation and desire. I would love one day to walk on the moon. But since I have no expectation of that ever happening I can't say, "I hope to walk on the moon." On the other hand, one day I am sure I will have to visit the dentist. But since I have no desire to visit the dentist it would be wrong to say, "I hope to visit the dentist." But as a Christian my greatest desire is to spend eternity with Jesus. And the promises of God make it absolutely certain that I will spend eternity with Jesus. So it is correct to say that my hope is spend eternity with Jesus.

This is not wishful thinking. This is the happy certainty of our Christian hope. And this promise is for every person who puts their trust in Jesus Christ who died and rose again; Jesus who said, *"I am the resurrection and the life. He who believes in me will live, even though he dies; and whoever lives and believes in me will never die."* (John 11:25-26)

PART 2

TALKING ABOUT JESUS

12 Be Prepared to Give an Answer

In Part 1 we have considered some of the questions people ask about faith and spiritual things. In Part 2 we will step back to think more generally about the important topic of talking about Jesus. Some Christians find it easy to share their faith with friends and neighbours and colleagues. But many find it difficult to do so and many wish they could be more confident and bold in talking about Jesus.

So why do Christians find it so hard to talk about Jesus? There are all sorts of reasons. One common fear is that of being rejected. We are scared of how the other person might react. We could be laughed at, or worse. Andrew Kirk wrote, "(Christians) are afraid of giving offence, causing embarrassment or being met with apathy, misunderstanding or ridicule. They may not wish to risk valued friendships. Perhaps the biggest cause of misgivings is the fear of being made to appear foolish, and thus of betraying their faith."[3] In other words, when it comes to talking about Jesus, many Christians are simply scared of getting it wrong. We don't know what to say. We are afraid we might do more harm than good. We might not be able to give answers to tricky questions. We are scared we might fail and let God down.

Some Christians are disillusioned because they have tried talking about Jesus before but feel they have failed. Some are afraid of taking risks. It has certainly become much harder than it used to be to talk about Jesus at work. We are understandably fearful of the potential consequences of witnessing for Christ in the workplace or in public places. We recognise that declaring that "Jesus is Lord" and that we are His disciples will sometimes carry many kinds of risks. Despite these pressures, the courageous witness of so many believers through history and around the world today gives us an inspiring example we need to learn to follow.

All these fears means that often many Christians leave evangelism to the professionals, to ministers and visiting evangelists and missionaries. But every Christian has a part to play in talking about Jesus. The Anglican evangelist Michael Green insists that the good news is too good to leave

---

[3] Andrew Kirk *Mission Under Scrutiny*, DLT 2006 91.

it to the professionals. He wrote, "Witness-bearing in some shape or form is the responsibility of all Christians."[4] In the Early Church, "every man and woman saw it as his task to bear witness to Jesus Christ by every means at his or her disposal."[5] The Bishop of Chelmsford evangelist Stephen Cottrell wrote, "According to our different personalities, gifts and circumstances each of us has a part to play in God's work of evangelism."[6] As Michael Green says, "It is not until church members have the enthusiasm to speak to their friends and acquaintances about Jesus that anybody will really believe we have got good news to share."[7]

It is the task of Ministers and Churches to encourage and equip all Christians to talk about Jesus wisely and boldly, confidently and effectively with anyone, wherever we may be. That is the purpose of this book.

In his first letter the apostle Peter was writing to Christians who were understandably scared of talking about Jesus. They were experiencing vicious persecution because of their faith. Peter wrote to them, *"Who is going to harm you if you are eager to do good? But even if you should suffer for what is right, you are blessed. Do not fear what they fear; do not be frightened."*
(1 Peter 3:13)
And then Peter gave them this encouragement.
"But in your hearts set apart Christ as Lord. Always be prepared to give an answer to everyone who asks you to give the reason for the hope that you have. But do this with gentleness and respect." (1 Peter 3:15)

Be prepared to give an answer. Help yourselves get ready to talk about Jesus. In his very practical advice, Peter began not with what we say but with how we live.

Set apart Christ as Lord in your hearts

Peter assumed that when Christians are living as Jesus wants us to then people will notice the difference. He wrote that God has made us into

---

[4] Michael Green *Evangelism Now and Then* IVP 1979 36.
[5] Michael Green *Evangelism Now and Then* IVP 1979 9.
[6] Stephen Cottrell *From the Abundance of the Heart* DLT 2006 20.
[7] Michael Green *Evangelism Now and Then* IVP 1979 35.

His people, *"called to proclaim the glory of god who called us out of darkness into his marvellous light."* (1 Peter 2:9-10)

In the Sermon on the Mount Jesus tells us that God has made Christians to be Salt and Light. He has made us to be a City set on a hill which cannot be hidden. The difference Jesus makes to our lives will cause people to ask questions. Early in the second century the Christian philosopher Justin Martyr wrote about the changed lives of Christians who,

> "changed their violent and tyrannical disposition, being overcome either by the constancy which they have witnessed in the lives of their Christian neighbours, or by the extraordinary forbearance they have observed in their Christian fellow travellers when defrauded, and by the honesty of those believers with whom they have transacted business."

As other people notice the difference Jesus makes to our lives, Christians then have an important responsibility.

Be prepared to give an answer

There are questions about faith Christians long for our friends to ask. What is a Christian? How can I become a Christian? What difference does being a Christian mean to you? What makes you sure God exists? In practice we may find that there are different questions in the minds of our friends and neighbours. Research summarised in *Evangelism in a Spiritual Age* [8] identified six Big Questions ordinary people are looking for answers to.

- Questions about Destiny: what happens after we die?
- Questions about Purpose: what is the point of life? What values should we live by? Who inspires us?
- Questions about the universe: how did it start? Is it designed or planned or controlled?
- Does God exist? What is he/it like? Can we know and have a relationship with God?

---

[8] *Evangelism in a Spiritual Age* editor Stephen Croft Church House Publishing 2005.

- Questions about Spiritual Realms: what form do they take? Questions about angels, ghosts, the supernatural and the paranormal.
- Questions about Suffering? Why is there so much? What can be done? This includes concerns about issues such as domestic abuse, crime, intolerance and lack of respect.

Christians need to be prepared to give an answer to the questions people are actually asking. Part 1 of this book is intended to help each of us to think through and develop our own answers to those kinds of questions.

Some people might think it is unspiritual to think through the kind of answers we might want to give in advance. However, the word 'answer' in 1 Peter 3:15 means more than just an "off the cuff" reply. The word translated answer, *apologia,* includes the idea of making a legal defence before a court, as the apostle Paul did a number of times in Acts 19, 22, 25 and 26. The word implies both the testimony a witness might give in court and also the arguments a lawyer might present in their opening and closing statements. We need to be ready to "give an answer" for the hope we have in Christ. In this, as in any situation where we have something very important we need to say, it is entirely appropriate to give thought in advance to the words we will use.

We may say to ourselves, "I am not an evangelist" It is true that few of us are ever called to preach the gospel to large groups of people at once, but "giving an answer" is not about public speaking. It is about engaging in conversations. Just talking about Jesus.

The Book of Acts talks about the first Christians preaching and proclaiming the gospel to huge crowds. But we also read about teaching and explaining and discussions and debates. Often we find Christians simply answering and replying to questions about their faith, convincing and persuading. We find them testifying and being witnesses to what they had seen and heard. We will think more about this this in chapter 14.

Furthermore, in Acts we see that it wasn't just the apostles and church leaders and the missionaries who talked about Jesus. It was also countless ordinary Christians who shared their faith. The majority of the talking about Jesus in the Early Church was done by people whose names we won't know this side of heaven.

On that day a great persecution broke out against the church at Jerusalem, and all except the apostles were scattered throughout Judea and Samaria. Godly men buried Stephen and mourned deeply for him. But Saul began to destroy the church. Going from house to house, he dragged off men and women and put them in prison. Those who had been scattered preached the word wherever they went. (Acts 8:1-4)

All these ordinary believers spread the Word of God with boldness, gossiping the gospel and chatting the good news not only in the synagogues but also with strangers in the marketplaces and with their friends in their own homes.

Now those who had been scattered by the persecution in connection with Stephen travelled as far as Phoenicia, Cyprus and Antioch, telling the message only to Jews. Some of them, however, men from Cyprus and Cyrene, went to Antioch and began to speak to Greeks also, telling them the good news about the Lord Jesus. The Lord's hand was with them, and a great number of people believed and turned to the Lord. (Acts 11:19-21)

Christians should all be prepared to give an answer. We need to start by listening carefully to our friends to discover what they really need to hear, so that we can say things which are appropriate for the stage in the journey to faith where our friend is at. As we talk about Jesus, what we say may take different forms. We may want to explain why we believe in Jesus. We may need to unpack some aspect of the Christian faith, answering the kind of questions we considered in Part 1. Sometimes we it may be appropriate to share a verse from the Bible or a story about Jesus. John 20:30-31 says, *Jesus did many other miraculous signs in the presence of his disciples, which are not recorded in this book. But these are written that you may believe that Jesus is the Christ, the Son of God, and that by believing you may have life in his name.* We believe that God can speak powerfully through His Word the Bible not only to believers but also to not yet Christians. Often our answer will therefore be simply to share what the Bible says. That is why it is a good thing for us to know by heart some Bible verses and to be able to retell some Bible stories about Jesus.

At other times it may be appropriate for Christians to talk about some part of our experience of God: answer to prayer; ways God has helped us; the difference Jesus makes to our lives; the hope or joy or peace Jesus gives us. It will help us to think through in advance what true life stories we want to be ready to tell to share our experiences of God. In particular, whenever we are talking about Jesus we will want to avoid using 'the language of Zion'; talking in jargon which only other Christians can understand. We want to think about the best words we can use which our friends and neighbours will understand as we share the wonderful truths of salvation and eternal life, faith and peace. We will think in more detail about the practicalities of sharing our story in chapter 16.

There is no need for us to present the whole gospel in one go – we never could anyway. We just need to share the little bit we are led to say at that time. The Holy Spirit can then take the whole jigsaw of things we have said and things other Christians have said and memories of school lessons and assemblies and bits of the Bible and a poster outside a church somewhere and fit together the full picture in the person's mind. We just need to supply our piece of the puzzle, our link in the chain. But we must be prepared to make the best of every precious opportunity.

Be wise in the way you act toward outsiders; make the most of every opportunity. Let your conversation be always full of grace, seasoned with salt, so that you may know how to answer everyone. (Colossians 4:5-6)
Use your heads as you live and work among outsiders. Don't miss a trick. Make the most of every opportunity. (The Message Translation of the same passage)

Of course, the manner in which we talk about Jesus is also very important. 1 Peter 3:15 goes on to say this.

Do so with courtesy and respect

We should never be preaching at people. We must always remember that "evangelism is one beggar telling another beggar where to find bread." The key is to be prepared. Prepared, as we need always to be prepared for the Lord's return like the wise virgins in Jesus's parable were. (Matthew 25:1-13) Prepared, like Paul was, to be bound and even to die for the sake of the gospel. (Acts 21:13) It is appropriate and indeed spiritual to prepare our answers. To think and pray in advance about what we might say, as a witness would prepare their testimony and answers to questions they expect to be asked. The motto of the Scout Movement is "Be prepared." How much more important and appropriate it is for Christians to be prepared to talk about Jesus.

John Finney's landmark book *Finding Faith Today*[9] reported that more than two thirds of Christians come to faith in a process which typically takes years rather than in one specific moment of decision. Friends and family members are the most significant contributors to that process. Research just published by the Barna Group reports that "44% of practising Christians credit their friends for introducing them to Jesus." More than a quarter of Christians say "conversation(s) with Christian(s) you knew well" and a further 9% say "conversation(s) with Christian(s) you did not know well" had a major impact on them coming to faith.[10]

Conversations about Jesus are vitally important. Most Christians recognise that truth – in theory at least. More than three quarters of practising Christians agree that "Talking to non-Christians about Jesus Christ is an act of evangelism".[11] 85% of practising Christians agree that "It is every Christian's responsibility to talk to non-Christians about Jesus." [12] However, when people who were not Christians were consulted, "More than half of non-Christians (54%) who know a Christian, have not had a conversation with this person about faith in Jesus. Two thirds (64%) of 45-54 year olds who know a practising Christian say they have never had a conversation with any practising Christian about their faith in Jesus Christ."[13]

Christians need to talk more about Jesus. Remember the sense of duty which the apostle Paul felt towards telling other people about Jesus.
Yet when I preach the gospel, I cannot boast, for I am compelled to preach. Woe to me if I do not preach the gospel! … · Though I am free and belong to no man, I make myself a slave to everyone, to win as many as possible. To the Jews I became like a Jew, to win the Jews. To those under the law I became like one under the law (though I myself am not under the law), so as to win those under the law. To those not having the law I became like one not having the law (though I am not free from God's law but

---

[9] John Finney *Finding Faith Today* BFBS 1992.
[10] *Talking Jesus* booklet p23 at www.talkingjesus.org.
[11] *Talking Jesus* booklet p13 at www.talkingjesus.org.
[12] *Talking Jesus* booklet p14 at www.talkingjesus.org.
[13] *Talking Jesus* booklet p21 at www.talkingjesus.org.

am under Christ's law), so as to win those not having the law. To the weak I became weak, to win the weak. I have become all things to all men so that by all possible means I might save some. (1 Corinthians 9:16,19-22)
Paul wrote about *using all possible means* to save people, doing whatever it takes, any which way we can. In this world of technology, talking about Jesus does not have to be face-to-face. Many Christians create wonderful opportunities to share their faith online, through blogs or via social media such as Facebook and Twitter. We may feel uneasy about the idea of 'evangelism'. There is an old story about an occasion when a lady criticised evangelist D.L Moody for his methods in proclaiming the gospel of Jesus Christ.
"I don't like the way you do it," she said.
"I agree with you," Moody answered. "I don't like the way I do it either. Tell me, how do you do it?"
"I don't do it," the lady replied.
Moody responded, "Then I like my way of doing it better than your way of not doing it."
Christians should be sharing the Good News of Jesus Christ any which way we can.

We need to talk more about Jesus. The evangelist Pete Gilbert gives this encouragement. "Potentially every good deed that you do, every good gift that you use, every good day that you inhabit, every good conversation that you have, every opportunity recognised and taken is a part of effective evangelism."[14] Michael Green wrote, "Personal conversation is the best way of evangelism. It is natural, it can be done anywhere, it can be done by anyone."[15] However we are led to do it, every church and every Christian needs to be making the very best of every opportunity to talk about Jesus.

Always be prepared to give an answer to everyone who asks you to give the reason for the hope that you have. (1 Peter 3:15)

---

[14] Pete Gilbert *Kiss and Tell Evangelism as a Lifestyle* CWR 2003 59.
[15] Michael Green *Evangelism Now and Then* IVP 1979 134.

13 Why we don't and why we should talk about Jesus

Some years ago we had the privilege of sharing in a Bible Study with the 18-30s group of a church in Sofia, the capital city of Bulgaria. They were looking at evangelism in Acts and somebody asked, "Suppose we were preaching the gospel in the square outside the (Eastern Orthodox) Cathedral and the police came and told us to stop preaching. Would we stop, or would we keep on preaching?" They agreed that they would keep on preaching, even though in the era of Communist rule, many Christians of their parents' generation actually had been arrested and imprisoned simply for preaching about Jesus in public. As indeed were many of the first Christians, but they were never deterred from talking about Jesus. *Day after day, in the temple courts and from house to house, they never stopped teaching and proclaiming the good news that Jesus is the Christ.* (Acts 5:42)

Those first Christians never stopped talking about Jesus. The problem for many Christians today is that we don't know how to start. Even facing brutal persecution, the Early Church would not be silenced. As Peter and John said to the Sanhedrin, *"Judge for yourselves whether it is right in God's sight to obey you rather than God. For we cannot help speaking about what we have seen and heard."* (Acts 4:19-20)

Today many Christians feel unprepared to share our faith. We are afraid that we don't know how to speak simply and directly about Jesus, or how to answer challenging questions. To address these anxieties, it is both appropriate and entirely spiritual to prepare in advance to give answers to particular questions, just as witnesses in court would prepare their testimony beforehand. It is right to take steps so that we are "prepared to give an answer" for our faith. Not only will we have a better idea of what we might say, but we will also be more vigilant and be more able to recognise openings to speak when they come. And then we will be more confident and bold to talk about Jesus and to discuss our faith.

There are so many important reasons why we would want to tell other people about Jesus. God has given us all the marvellous blessings of salvation. Our sins are forgiven so we can have a relationship with God our loving heavenly Father. We have received the free gift of eternal life, life in all its fullness which begins here and how and will continue in heaven forever. So we are indebted to God. We are so grateful for the grace He has poured into lives and for the love, joy and peace we experience day by day.in our relationship with Jesus. We want to show our gratitude by talking about Jesus whenever we can.

Then we have been commissioned and sent by Jesus to preach the Good News.
"Therefore go and make disciples of all nations, baptizing them in the name of the Father and of the Son and of the Holy Spirit." (Matthew 28:19)
"Go into all the world and preach the good news to all creation." (Mark 16:15)

Jesus gives all His disciples the wonderful promise of the Holy Spirit, God Himself living inside every Christian – and note that this is not a command but is indeed a promise.
"You will receive power when the Holy Spirit comes on you; and you will be my witnesses in Jerusalem, and in all Judea and Samaria, and to the ends of the earth." (Acts 1:8)

It is the Holy Spirit Who initiates, leads, guides and empowers Christians in evangelism. Throughout the book of Acts, the Early Church give us continual examples of their witness. God gives to all Christians the responsibility of being His Ambassadors. And we are also motivated to talk about Jesus because we are moved to love with God's love both friends and strangers, who the Bible tells us are lost and even dead without Christ. Last, but by no means least, the most fundamental reason for preaching the gospel is found within the gospel itself. It is a message so important that it deserves and demands to be passed on. So why do we not?

Some Christians are unsure of what the gospel, the Good News about Jesus Christ, actually is. Part of being "prepared to give an answer" is to be sure of what the gospel is and to be able to explain it in terms which not yet Christian people can relate to and understand. Then we need to have in mind the kinds of answers we could give to the kinds of questions people might ask us. That was the content of Part 1.

However nowadays there are some Christians who suggest we should not need to tell other people about Jesus. They say that if we are living Christ-like lives then it should not be necessary for us actually to tell anybody the gospel. We will think about that in the next chapter. Such ideas are mistaken. The truth is that sharing the Good News will always require words. Talking about Jesus is not an optional extra.

Some misguided people are also rejecting literal understandings of hell and eternal judgement. There is this growing idea that "love wins" and so "everybody will be saved" in the end. Some mistakenly feel that, if nobody is ultimately lost, why do we need to talk about Jesus at all? Those ideas are also wrong. As we have discussed earlier, *all have sinned and fall short of God's glory.* (Romans 3:23) However we may understand the teaching on hell, the Bible makes clear in so many places that our friends and neighbours and colleagues really do still need God to save them. Everybody needs to hear the message of Good News.

There are many other reasons why Christians find it hard to talk about Jesus. There are pressures from society making it less acceptable to talk about our faith. It is considered politically incorrect to challenge somebody else's opinion. It is not easy to proclaim that Jesus Christ is unique, the only way to God and the only source of salvation. These claims can sound arrogant and even rude, even though we know they are true.

Some Christians have never tried talking about Jesus to their friends before and are understandably nervous about starting. Some are disillusioned with sharing their faith because they have tried before but feel that they failed and are afraid of failing again. Others are afraid of taking risks or of losing friends. Recent highly publicised judgments of industrial tribunals and of courts have been disappointing in penalising some Christians who have been bold enough to share their faith. So it is completely reasonable to be scared of the potential consequences of witnessing for Christ in the workplace or in public places.

It may appear difficult for Christians today to talk about Jesus, but we should keep in mind that it was very much harder for those first Christians to declare that "Jesus is Lord" in a society where people were only permitted to say, "Caesar is Lord". Telling other people that we are

followers of Jesus will sometimes carry risks. The courageous witness of countless believers through history and so many around the world still today puts many of us to shame. They talk about Jesus even though it may cost them their freedom or even their lives. And the words of Jesus also challenge us.
For whoever wants to save his life will lose it, but whoever loses his life for me will save it. What good is it for a man to gain the whole world, and yet lose or forfeit his very self? If anyone is ashamed of me and my words, the Son of Man will be ashamed of him when he comes in his glory and in the glory of the Father and of the holy angels. (Luke 9:24-26)

We have all these important reasons why we should be talking to our friends and neighbours and colleagues about Jesus. But there are also all these kinds of discouragements which mean that often we don't. We may we anxious about talking about Jesus. We may be afraid. Being prepared to give an answer will help us set aside our fears. And we need to put our trust in God. God, the Holy Spirit Himself, is living and working inside us!
For God did not give us a spirit of timidity, but a spirit of power, of love and of self-discipline. So do not be ashamed to testify about our Lord, or ashamed of me his prisoner. (2 Timothy 1:7-8)

God gives us the Holy Spirit to help us to be His witnesses. God does not want us to be worried or afraid about speaking for Him. Jesus knew what His disciples would face and He promised them the power of the Holy Spirit.
"You must be on your guard. You will be handed over to the local councils and flogged in the synagogues. On account of me you will stand before governors and kings as witnesses to them. And the gospel must first be preached to all nations. Whenever you are arrested and brought to trial, do not worry beforehand about what to say. Just say whatever is given you at the time, for it is not you speaking, but the Holy Spirit." (Mark 13:9-11)

If we are worried or scared about talking about Jesus, we need to release the power of the Holy Spirit by praying. Talking about Jesus must start in prayer, and talking about Jesus must continue surrounded in prayer. Prayer is obviously so important that we will devote a whole chapter to it soon.

14 Preaching the gospel necessarily includes using words

Sometime in the 1990s a striking saying became popular. "Preach the gospel and if necessary use words." Widely quoted, attributed to Francis of Assisi, and riding on his reputation, it seemed to fit the mood of Christians who were disaffected with evangelism as it had been practised in the Twentieth Century. But the slogan is fatally flawed.

Evangelist Pete Gilberts observes that the phrase, "if necessary use words," is used by some Christians as a "get-out clause",[16] as if somehow that saying alone allows them to stay silent about their faith. Roman Catholic blogger Emily Stimpson explains the problem very clearly. "Someone invented the quote and put it into poor St. Francis' mouth. And ever since then, people have used it as an excuse to not evangelize with words, to not have the uncomfortable conversations or say the unpopular things."[17]

Some writers even use the saying to suggest that Christians have somehow failed in their witness if their daily lives are so inadequate that they need to articulate the gospel in words. Unhelpfully this can leave some Christians feeling guilty when they do talk about Jesus. But any suggestion that our actions should be sufficient and that words should not be necessary in evangelism is gravely mistaken.

Francis never said that!

This point needs to be made very strongly. Saint Francis never said, "if necessary use words". Drawing on his own biography of Francis, Mark Galli wrote in *Christianity Today* that no early sources contain the quote or anything like it. Nor in his view is it the kind of thing Francis would have been likely to say. "In his day, Francis was known as much for his preaching as for his lifestyle. … He soon took up itinerant ministry,

---

[16] Pete Gilbert *Kiss and Tell* 111.

[17] Emily Stimpson http://www.catholicvote.org/pope-francis-and-st-francis-preach-the-gospel-always-and-for-the-love-of-god-use-words/.

sometimes preaching in up to five villages a day, often outdoors … He preached to serfs and their families as well as to the landholders, to merchants, women, clerks, and priests"[18]

Emily Stimpson says the same. "Every chance Francis got, he proclaimed the Gospel. He proclaimed it to the wolves in the forest. He proclaimed it to the Sultan in Egypt. He wouldn't stop talking about Jesus. He couldn't. Anymore than a woman in love can stop talking about her beloved. The thought of not speaking about his love, about Christ, to the world, would have horrified the little Poverello." "He knew what the Church has always known. There is no "if" about the necessity of words in evangelization, just as there is no "if" about the necessity of actions. They are both necessary. They are both essential." "Preach the gospel. Since it is necessary, use words"[19]

Evangelism in the New Testament

In the Bible, as we have seen, the gospel is the message of Good News about Jesus Christ: the declaration that Jesus Christ is risen from the dead and he is Lord and that God offers forgiveness, eternal life and all the blessings of salvation to everyone who puts their trust in Jesus. All the verbs used for the ways the first Christians passed on that message are aspects of speech: preaching; proclaiming; teaching; testifying and more which we will discuss below. The book of Acts is very interested in the way "the word" spread (Acts 6:7; 12:24; 13:49; 19:20). The apostle Paul argues that people can only be saved if somebody preaches to them "the word of faith" (Romans 10:8-15). Christians are called to be ambassadors for Christ (2 Corinthians 5:18-21) and that role will always include delivering their Sovereign's messages. The historical fact that the first Christians all experienced fierce persecution is evidence enough that they were indeed proclaiming the good news with boldness.

The church has always understood evangelism that way. His Holiness Pope Paul VI pronounced,

---

18 Mark Galli "*Speak* the Gospel: Use deeds when necessary." *Christianity Today* May 21, 2009.

19 Emily Stimpson as above.

> "Nevertheless [witness] always remains insufficient, because even the finest witness will prove ineffective in the long run if it is not explained, justified…and made explicit by a clear and unequivocal proclamation of the Lord Jesus. The Good News proclaimed by the witness of life sooner or later has to be proclaimed by the word of life. There is no true evangelization if the name, the teaching, the life, the promises, the kingdom and the mystery of Jesus of Nazareth, the Son of God are not proclaimed."[20]

In his landmark book, *The logic of evangelism*, William Abraham is equally clear.

> "We need to emphasise that by 'proclamation of the gospel' we mean the *verbal* (his italics) proclamation, in order to prevent evangelism from sliding into a thoroughly vague notion that stands for everything and anything that the church does in witness and service."[21]

Christians are sent by God to share the Good News of Jesus. In some corners of the church it seems as if the heralds have been struck dumb and the messengers have forgotten the message. We really do need to talk about Jesus.

So how should we preach the gospel?

"Preach the gospel and if necessary use words" has become popular in part because it offers a valuable reminder that our deeds must match our words. Our lives must back up our message. It is undeniable that "they won't care what we know until they know that we care" Thankfully most strands of the church have recognised this fact and moved increasingly towards "integral mission", proclaiming and demonstrating the gospel side by side. "Mission is being, doing and telling." (Dean Flemming) Christians should love our neighbours by serving our communities and by striving for compassion, justice and peace. But this love should always go hand in hand with delivering the Good News of Jesus in words. Tim Chester is right to comment, "It is not enough merely to address people's

---

[20] Pope Paul VI *Evangelii Nuntiandi* (encyclical on evangelization) 1974.
[21] William Abraham *The Logic of Evangelism* 44.

felt needs. As well as their temporal needs we must also address their eternal need of Christ."[22]

Another reason the phrase "if necessary use words" seems to resonate for many people is that the image of evangelism has been tarnished by many factors, including by outdated and embarrassing methods, by poor literature, by approaches which appear manipulative or insensitive to other cultures and by the greed of disgraced televangelists. Additionally, many Christians have been discouraged by experiences of evangelistic programmes and events which have appeared to fail. Stuart Murray is right to suggest, "Rehabilitating and reconfiguring evangelism are crucial but attainable tasks on the threshold of post-Christendom."[23]

The idea that it is possible to "preach the gospel" without using words is completely mistaken. At the same time, changes in the world around us challenge the church to reflect on the words we use, our attitudes and the stance we should take in evangelism and on the forms of communication we use to share the gospel.

Sociologists tell us that society in the United Kingdom has become more and more multi-faith and multicultural, Post-Modern and Post-Christendom. Many people have rejected not only Christian values but also any concept of absolute truth. For very many people, truth is no longer regarded as something which is objective, rooted in fact, but rather as subjective, rooted in experience and consequently different for each person. Nowadays we are told that the only thing we can be certain of is that we aren't allowed to be certain about anything anymore. It is seen as politically incorrect to challenge somebody else's opinion. As a result, proclaiming that Jesus Christ is unique, the only way to God (John 14:6) and the only source of salvation (Acts 4:12) can appear to be ill-mannered and even arrogant.

Bishop Lesslie Newbigin emphasised that the Christian's authority for mission comes "in the Name of Jesus" (Matthew 28:18-19) as Christ sends us out with a life-or-death message. We don't have to be able to prove to a certainty that our religious claims are true. Good reasons are

---

[22] Tim Chester *Mission Matters* 100.

[23] Stuart Murray *Post-Christendom* 226.

sufficient. So we must not compromise and we dare not be silent. Andrew Kirk describes evangelism as "the process of communicating the most crucial piece of knowledge possible about real life in such a way that the recipient has the maximum opportunity to understand and act upon it."[24] Fundamentally, the mandate for preaching the gospel is found within that most important message – so vital that it deserves and demands to be passed on. As Walter Brueggemann wrote, it is "the simple 'news' of the gospel itself that provides a missionary impetus for sharing the news with our 'news starved' society. Finally, the ground of evangelism is found in the gospel itself, and not in any church condition or societal need."[25] The gospel contains within itself our authority for proclaiming it.

In talking about Jesus, Christians are not claiming to be superior to other people. Christians do believe that we have an understanding of life which is missing in other faiths but reaching that truth is not an achievement worthy of praise but rather a revelation, a gift from God (Ephesians 2:8-9). So it is not arrogant or conceited or self-righteousness to claim to have discovered that truth. It is offered to everyone as a free gift.

Having said that, Christians need to recognise that the church is not the centre of society any more. We are speaking "from the edge." Most folk have very little knowledge of the Bible or of the life and teaching of Jesus, which were presupposed in the evangelistic approach of Billy Graham and to some extent in courses like Alpha and Christianity Explored. More than that, we must keep in mind that many people have rejected Christianity on all sorts of grounds as old fashioned, irrelevant, patriarchal, homophobic, authoritarian, judgmental and hypocritical and expressing an outdated morality, causing wars, persecuting opponents and abusing the planet.[26]

We live in a consumer society, "Tesco ergo Sum, I shop therefore I am" (Graham Cray). People demand freedom of choice and satisfaction guaranteed. In this Post-Modern supermarket of beliefs, "the preacher can become another dodgy salesperson almost certainly out to con

---

[24] Andrew Kirk *Mission Under Scrutiny* 103.

[25] Walter Brueggemann *Biblical Perspectives on Evangelism.*

[26] Steve Hollinghurst, *Mission Shaped Evangelism* 190.

you."[27] For all the reasons above, we Christians must change our attitudes and our stance in our evangelism. Stuart Murray suggests this will require "renouncing imperialist language and cultural imposition, making truth claims with humility and respecting other viewpoints."[28] We must remember that we are only ever "one beggar telling another beggar where to find bread." We must recognise how alien church and Christian things can appear, avoid "the language of Zion" and express the Good News in words and images and stories which our neighbours can actually understand. We need to think through how we will talk about Jesus.

How was the Good News shared in the New Testament?

Nowadays the very word "preaching" carries negative connotations for many people. "Don't preach at me!" When we consider Jesus preaching and teaching we immediately think of the Sermon on the Mount and of Jesus speaking to crowds. We can forget that very much of Jesus's teaching was given just to the twelve apostles, and some exclusively to his inner circle of Peter, James and John. Over the three years of his ministry, Jesus must surely also have had countless unrecorded one-to-one conversations with every one of his apostles.

More than that, the New Testament includes the details of many significant conversations which Jesus had with individuals, many of whom would still have been alive when the Gospels were written. Just in John's Gospel we find Jesus talking with Andrew, with Simon Peter, with Philip and with Nathanael (all in chapter 1) with Nicodemus (John 3) with the Samaritan Woman at the Well and with a Royal Official (John 4) with a Paralysed Man (John 5) with a Woman Caught in Adultery (John 8) with a Man who was Born Blind (John 9) with Martha and with Mary (John 11) and with Pontius Pilate (John 18). Other Gospels record memorable conversations between Jesus and the Rich Young Ruler, a Centurion, the Father of a dead girl, a Sick Woman and Simon the Pharisee, as well as with many of the people he healed, with a number of inquirers and with various would-be disciples. In passing, each of these encounters gives valuable insights regarding approaches Christians might take when we are talking about Jesus, sharing the Good News or

27 Steve Hollinghurst *Mission Shaped Evangelism* 161.

28 Stuart Murray *Post-Christendom* 229.

discussing faith and spiritual topics. The overall point to recognise is that Jesus himself frequently taught and proclaimed the Good News with twos and threes and often in private conversations one-to-one. We are not limited to following the example of Jesus in our outreach, but it is surely a good place to start.

Similarly, in Acts public preaching and proclamation were not the only ways that the gospel was communicated. Luke recorded the patterns of evangelism we see in Acts to give us examples of what Christians through the ages could, and probably often should, be doing. There we see that sometimes the gospel was preached (17 times) or proclaimed (10 times) to large groups. But there was also debate (twice) and teaching (10 times) both in public and in private homes (Acts 20:28). Sometimes we see small groups and one-to-one conversations (e.g. Philip in Acts 8:26). Christians explained the gospel (5 times) and attempted to persuade or convince (4 times). Often they did not even need to initiate the conversations. On 10 occasions we find them answering or replying to questions. Sometimes they pointed to Scripture and on other occasions they simply testified (6 times) or acted as witnesses (9 times) regarding their personal experiences. In passing, this gives us a list of at least 74 instances of verbal communication in Acts when the first Christians evidently found it necessary to use words to communicate the gospel. But less than one third of those occasions involved preaching or proclaiming: more often Christians were simply having conversations about Jesus.

Dialogue reaches the hearts monologue can't reach

A long time ago I came up with a simple slogan for the world of education. "Dialogue teaches the parts monologue can't teach." In evangelism I would phrase it slightly differently. "Dialogue reaches the hearts monologue can't reach." Very often the best way to convey the gospel message today will be through dialogue, by engaging in conversations which explore spirituality and share faith, by teaching and explaining, persuading, convincing, sharing Scripture, and frequently just by answering questions. In all of this we are not only seeking to reach the minds of our friends, but opening a way for God to touch their hearts.

Stuart Murray has written that evangelism should become "Engaging in conversation rather than confrontation – evangelism alongside others, not declaiming from an authoritative height, through dialogue instead of monologue."[29] "Gentle questioning must supersede domineering assertions. Bold humility must replace arrogant insecurity. The images of fellow travellers and conversation partners must usurp memories of inquisitors and crusaders."[30]

Someone might object that dialogue is not an appropriate approach since Christians have already decided the message they want to convey and the conclusions they want others to reach. But in all areas of life dialogue will often involve elements of persuasion and that is as legitimate in talking about Jesus as it is anywhere else, as long as we are always open, direct, honest, caring and never manipulative.

I fervently hope never to hear or read again the saying we began with. None of us can hide behind it. Of course Christians are allowed to talk about Jesus. More than that, the Bible makes clear that it will always be appropriate for every Christian to express the life-saving Good News of Jesus in words as well as in actions. No trendy slogan will ever give us permission to be silent. We all need to make the best of every opportunity for conversations about Jesus.

---

[29] Stuart Murray *Post-Christendom* 230.
[30] Stuart Murray *Post-Christendom* 231.

15 Praying about talking about Jesus

"But you will receive power when the Holy Spirit comes on you; and you will be my witnesses in Jerusalem, and in all Judea and Samaria, and to the ends of the earth." (Acts 1:8)

Jesus made such wonderful promises to all His disciples. One of the most precious is this promise of the gift of the Holy Spirit, power from on high, power to be witnesses for Jesus. It is very important that Christians remember in all our talking about Jesus, in all our outreach and witness and evangelism, that there is absolutely nothing we can do to save people. That is entirely the work of God the Holy Spirit. We know that it is only the Holy Spirit who can bring somebody to eternal life in Christ. It is the Holy Spirit who helps people to understand the Bible. It is the Holy Spirit who convicts people of sin. It is the Holy Spirit who helps people to put their trust in Jesus. It is the Holy Spirit who brings a person to new birth and gives them new life and helps them to believe that Jesus is risen from the dead and to declare that Jesus Christ is Lord. It is the Holy Spirit who makes us God's children and who makes each of us part of the Body of Christ, the church.

You will receive power … and you will be my witnesses. Believers through the centuries have claimed and experienced this promise for themselves. The Greek word for power is *dunamis* from which we get the English words dynamic, dynamo and dynamite. God the Holy Spirit is the dynamic, the dynamo and the dynamite of Christian living and especially of witness and evangelism. When it comes to talking about Jesus, as in every other area of our Christian lives, we know God's words in Zechariah 4:6 are true. *"Not by might nor by power, but by my Spirit," says the LORD Almighty.* It is not us but it is the Holy Spirit who is the principal witness to Jesus and to the gospel. So we need to pray that God will release the Holy Spirit into our lives and into our church.

Peter and the other apostles replied: "We must obey God rather than men! The God of our fathers raised Jesus from the dead—whom you had killed by hanging him on a tree. God exalted him to his own right hand as Prince and Saviour that he might give repentance and forgiveness of sins to Israel. We are witnesses of these things, and so is the Holy Spirit, whom God has given to those who obey him." (Acts 5:29-32)

The Holy Spirit is the witness and then God will help us as we are witnesses for Him. The way we release the power of God into our outreach and evangelism is of course by praying.

And pray in the Spirit on all occasions with all kinds of prayers and requests. With this in mind, be alert and always keep on praying for all the saints. Pray also for me, that whenever I open my mouth, words may be given me so that I will fearlessly make known the mystery of the gospel, for which I am an ambassador in chains. Pray that I may declare it fearlessly, as I should. (Ephesians 6:18-20)

The apostle Paul was asking the Ephesian Christians to pray for him that he might be a faithful ambassador for Jesus. He asked them to pray that he might talk about Jesus without being afraid. If the apostle Paul needed people to pray those things for him, then we do even more. We should be praying those kind of prayers for ourselves and for each other. Especially if we are scared or worried about talking about Jesus, we should pray about that. Paul also asked the Colossians to pray for his witness for Jesus.

Devote yourselves to prayer, being watchful and thankful. And pray for us, too, that God may open a door for our message, so that we may proclaim the mystery of Christ, for which I am in chains. Pray that I may proclaim it clearly, as I should. (Colossians 4:2-4)

Here Paul asked other Christians to pray for him, that God will open doors for him to talk about Jesus and that he will be clear in what he says when he does. We can pray those things for ourselves and for each other; very specific prayers that God will give us opportunities for conversations about Jesus. Paul continues,

Be wise in the way you act toward outsiders; make the most of every opportunity. Let your conversation be always full of grace, seasoned with salt, so that you may know how to answer everyone. (Colossians 4:5-6)

We pray about our witness, that God will give us opportunities to talk about Jesus and that He will enable us to make the most of every opportunity. We pray to know how to give good answers to everyone. Witness, outreach and evangelism must start in prayer, and must continue surrounded in prayer. We need prayer which includes both listening for God to guide our witness and also interceding for ourselves and for others.

We should pray for ourselves, especially for boldness. Even the Early Church needed to pray for courage to speak out about Jesus, and God answered their prayers.

"Now, Lord, consider their threats and enable your servants to speak your word with great boldness. Stretch out your hand to heal and perform miraculous signs and wonders through the name of your holy servant Jesus."
After they prayed, the place where they were meeting was shaken. And they were all filled with the Holy Spirit and spoke the word of God boldly. (Acts 4:29-31)

God puts His Holy Spirit inside us so that when we talk about Jesus we will be able to be bold and not fearful.

For God did not give us a spirit of timidity, but a spirit of power, of love and of self-discipline. So do not be ashamed to testify about our Lord, or ashamed of me his prisoner. (2 Timothy 1:7)

We should also pray for wisdom, to know what to say and what answers to give.

If any of you lacks wisdom, he should ask God, who gives generously to all without finding fault, and it will be given to him. (James 1:5)

We will pray about our outreach strategy and outreach events and special services. We pray about our organised evangelism but we should also be praying individually and together that God will give each of us opportunities to talk about Jesus and that He will enable us to make the most of every opportunity and answer everyone the best we can.

We should continually be praying for our friends and our neighbours and our colleagues. There is a wise saying, "Always talk to God about your friend before you talk to your friend about God." We can pray for other people. We often think of praying for our friends' physical needs but we should also keep on praying that they will be able to understand the Good News of Jesus. When appropriate we can tell other people we are praying for them and ask them what they would like us to pray for them. We pray and persevere in praying for specific individuals that they will be saved. We should pray in our personal times of prayer, in Home Groups and Cell Groups, in special prayer meetings and in days and nights of prayer, and sometimes praying with fasting. If we are serious about sharing the Good News of Jesus Christ we will take every opportunity to pray.

We should never forget that there is a spiritual dimension to talking about Jesus.

And even if our gospel is veiled, it is veiled to those who are perishing. The god of this age has blinded the minds of unbelievers, so that they cannot see the light of the gospel of the glory of Christ, who is the image of God. For we do not preach ourselves, but Jesus Christ as Lord, and ourselves as your servants for Jesus' sake. For God, who said, "Let light shine out of darkness," made his light shine in our hearts to give us the light of the knowledge of the glory of God in the face of Christ.
(2 Corinthians 4:3-4)

Talking about Jesus is a challenge to *the god of this age* who *has blinded the minds of unbelievers.* There will be spiritual opposition when we talk about Jesus. But we should not be afraid. Jesus has overcome all the powers of darkness. Fully one third of the miracles Jesus performed were acts of deliverance, as the Kingly Rule of God drove out the powers of evil.

Jesus knew their thoughts and said to them, "Every kingdom divided against itself will be ruined, and every city or household divided against itself will not stand. If Satan drives out Satan, he is divided against himself. How then can his kingdom stand? And if I drive out demons by Beelzebub, by whom do your people drive them out? So then, they will be your judges. But if I drive out demons by the Spirit of God, then the kingdom of God has come upon you. Or again, how can anyone enter a strong man's house and carry off his possessions unless he first ties up the strong man? Then he can rob his house. (Matthew 12:25-29)

Jesus "bound the strong man" when he resisted the temptations in his forty days in the wilderness. Jesus then defeated the devil by his death on the cross. And Jesus has delegated His authority over all the powers of evil to his church

I will give you the keys of the kingdom of heaven; whatever you bind on earth will be bound in heaven, and whatever you loose on earth will be loosed in heaven."
(Matthew 16:19)

So talking about Jesus has a deeply spiritual dimension. Sometimes a conversation about Jesus will be a spiritual battle. We need to be praying.

Prayer walking

When we are making plans to share the Good News of Jesus beyond the circle of our own friends and neighbours and colleagues, we need to prepare the ground for outreach by prayer. One way we can do this is by Prayer Walking. We do not have to be in a church building for God to answer our prayers. We do not need to be on our knees or have our eyes closed for God to answer our prayers. The more we know about other people and can empathise with their needs the easier we find it to pray meaningfully for them. Prayer walking is simply praying as we walk around our neighbourhood.

Some people date the first account of prayer walking to 467 AD when the Bishop of Vienne in France led processions around the boundary of the town to seek God's blessing. The festival of 'Rogantide', from the Latin for asking or interceding, became part of the Roman Catholic calendar. Then by the Middle Ages, "beating the bounds" of the parish was an important event in the life of the church. The priest would lead the congregation around the boundaries of the parish declaring blessings and praying. People would literally "beat the bounds" with branches, believing that this would drive demons out of the parish. These seemingly strange historical practices may well show us a neglected truth.

Part of prayer walking is simply praying God's blessing on the homes we pass. We believe that praying for people works. More than that, we also believe that Christians can declare God's blessings on each other and on the community. In the Old Testament the priests were appointed by God to declare His blessing and His peace on His people. (Numbers 6:22-27) Jesus sent out the Twelve (Matthew 10:5-15) and the Seventy-two (Luke 10:1-12) to heal, to minister deliverance and to preach the gospel. Jesus commanded them in Luke 10:5, *"When you enter a house, first say, `Peace to this house.' If a man of peace is there, your peace will rest on him; if not, it will return to you."* In the priesthood of all believers, every Christian is empowered to act as God's representative and proclaim God's blessing. In Prayer Walking we can both pray for the homes and the people we are passing and also declare God's peace and blessing upon them.

Then we are also listening to God as we walk. God gives spiritual gifts of prophecy, discernment, knowledge and wisdom to His church. The Holy Spirit at work in every Christian allows all of us to hear God's voice and be led by Him. So part of prayer walking is listening to God so that we will know more precisely what to pray for (Romans 8:26-27). We listen for specific guidance about the approaches we should take to outreach and evangelism, and for discernment about the presence of evil in particular places. Beyond asking God's blessing, listening to God and expressing our faith, prayer walking is also an activity of spiritual warfare.

Joshua 6 tells us of the battle of Jericho; a battle which the Israelites did not need to fight because God gave them the victory. But the Israelites were not passive there. They were obedient: by marching around the city they were demonstrating their faith in God. Even when they did not understand what God was commanding them to do, they trusted and they obeyed. Similarly, prayer walking is an expression of faith and obedience. And God will honour that. We might find it easier instead to deliver leaflets or knock on doors. We could be tempted into thinking that activities of explicit evangelism would achieve more. But prayer walking is an expression of our faith in God and a recognition that only the Holy Spirit can bring people to Christ.

All prayer is an exercise in faith. We should be praying for all our evangelism and outreach and witness. Praying for ourselves. Praying for the people we want to share Jesus with. Praying about talking about Jesus. Many Christians like to feel busy. We can so easily be tempted to put our trust in human activity. Absolutely the most important thing we can be doing is to pray and to pray and keep on praying. *"Not by might nor by power, but by my Spirit," says the LORD Almighty.*

A postscript on spiritual warfare

The experience of churches in many parts of the world suggests that certain places can be particularly influenced by evil spirits as a result of activities there in the past or present. Some writers describe these as 'territorial spirits.' In prayer walking, Christians are proclaiming Christ's victory and claiming the ground. If you are not familiar with those aspects of prayer, this short explanation may be helpful.

The reason the Son of God appeared was to destroy the devil's work. (1 John 3:8) Part of prayer walking is simply praising God and declaring Jesus's victory over all the powers of evil. We are also seeking the Holy Spirit's guidance in discerning whether evil powers have any claim over any particular places or people. This may lead us on to specific prayers for deliverance. This is one way we can fulfil Jesus's commission to His church, not only to proclaim the gospel but also to bring healing and deliverance. *"As you go, preach this message: 'The kingdom of heaven is near.' Heal the sick, raise the dead, cleanse those who have leprosy, drive out demons."* (Matthew 10:7-8)

There is evidence in the Bible to support the idea of 'territorial spirits' as many churches and missionaries understand them. The Bible describes the devil or Satan as *"the prince of this world"* (John 12:31) and *"the God of this age (who) has blinded the minds of unbelievers"* (2 Corinthians 4:4). The tenth plague on Egypt of the deaths of the firstborn was, in God's words, *"judgement on all the gods of Egypt"* (Exodus 12:12). The opposition of *"the prince of Persia"* to God's angel recorded in Daniel 10:12-13 implies an evil spirit controlling an area. Similarly, it appears that there may well have been specific demons behind the earthly kings of Babylon and Tyre (Isaiah 14:12-14, Ezekiel 28:12-16). The demons in Legion seemed to fear being sent out of 'their' region (Mark 5:1-20). Pergamum was the place *"where Satan's throne is"* (Revelation 2:13) which may imply not merely a pagan temple but behind that a level of demonic control. The Old Testament teaches that the sins of the fathers will be visited on the children (Leviticus 26:39, Jeremiah 32:18) even to the fourth generation (Exodus 20:5, 34:7, Numbers 14:18). This can sometimes happen through demons gaining a hold on families. We should also be aware that witchcraft and magic, curses and spells do have real power to harm people.[31]

While it is appropriate to be aware of the possibility of spiritual opposition as we talk about Jesus, Christians have nothing to fear. On the cross Christ has triumphed over all the powers of evil. *Having disarmed the powers and authorities, he made a public spectacle of them, triumphing over them by the cross.* (Colossians 2:15) In the name of Jesus, we have the victory!

---

[31]This understanding of spiritual warfare and territorial spirits is explained in several books by church growth expert Peter Wagner including *Territorial Spirits*, *Breaking Strongholds in Your City*, *Wrestling with Dark Angels* and *Engaging the Enemy*. See also John Dawson *Taking our Cities for God.*

16 Sharing my story

In this multi-faith, multicultural, consumer society, many people have become suspicious of authority figures and platform speakers. On the other hand, they are often willing and eager to share "their story" and equally open to hearing "our story", especially from their friends. So every Christian needs to be prepared to talk simply, directly and honestly, about the difference Jesus makes to our lives. We need to be ready to act as witnesses; to give testimony about what we have seen and heard and experienced. Mark Cartledge defines Christian testimony like this. "People tell of their need and desire for God and His Kingdom, how God has met and continues to meet them in their search and changes their lives in conformity with His purposes of salvation."[32]

In the Early Church the primary task of the apostles was to bear witness to the resurrection of Jesus. This is what Jesus had commanded them to do.

"When the Counsellor comes, whom I will send to you from the Father, the Spirit of truth who goes out from the Father, he will testify about me. And you also must testify, for you have been with me from the beginning." (John 15:26-27)

With great power the apostles continued to testify to the resurrection of the Lord Jesus, and much grace was upon them all. (Acts 4:33)

"The God of our fathers raised Jesus from the dead … God exalted him to his own right hand as Prince and Saviour that he might give repentance and forgiveness of sins to Israel. We are witnesses of these things, and so is the Holy Spirit, whom God has given to those who obey him." (Acts 5:30-32)

The word witness occurs 69 times in the New Testament. God the Holy Spirit empowers all Christians to be witnesses, helping us to tell other people what we have experienced of God.

"But you will receive power when the Holy Spirit comes on you; and you will be my witnesses in Jerusalem, and in all Judea and Samaria, and to the ends of the earth." (Acts 1:8)

---

[32]Mark Cartledge *Testimony Its importance, place and potential* Grove Renewal 9 2002 3.

In the New Testament there are many examples of believers telling other people the story of how they met Jesus. The apostle Peter only came to know Jesus because of the testimony of his brother Andrew.
Andrew, Simon Peter's brother, was one of the two who heard what John had said and who had followed Jesus. The first thing Andrew did was to find his brother Simon and tell him, "We have found the Messiah" (that is, the Christ). And he brought him to Jesus. (John 1:40-42)

We read that the first thing Matthew did after Jesus called him was to hold a dinner party and invite all his friends to meet Jesus, even "tax collectors and sinners". (Matthew 9:9-13) We can do similarly. When Jesus drove a Legion of demons out of a man and into a herd of pigs, everybody who knew the man saw the dramatic change in his life. And the man was so full of joy he couldn't stop telling everybody that it was Jesus who had set him free (Mark 5:18-20).

When Jesus met a Samaritan woman by a well he talked to her about the water which wells up to eternal life. He invited her to call her husband knowing that she did not have one. She recognised that Jesus was a prophet and wondered if he could even be the Messiah the Jews were expecting. So she went and told her neighbours. They came to Jesus and put their trust in him too.
Then, leaving her water jar, the woman went back to the town and said to the people, "Come, see a man who told me everything I ever did. Could this be the Christ?" They came out of the town and made their way toward him. …
Many of the Samaritans from that town believed in him because of the woman's testimony, "He told me everything I ever did." So when the Samaritans came to him, they urged him to stay with them, and he stayed two days. And because of his words many more became believers. They said to the woman, "We no longer believe just because of what you said; now we have heard for ourselves, and we know that this man really is the Saviour of the world." (John 4:28-30, 39-42)

In John 9 we read how Jesus healed a man who had been born blind. That man bears witness to his experience of healing in a number of stages. Initially he just explains what has happened to him.
So the man went and washed, and came home seeing. His neighbours and those who had formerly seen him begging asked, "Isn't this the same man who used to sit and beg?" Some claimed that he was. Others said, "No, he only looks like him."
But he himself insisted, "I am the man."

"How then were your eyes opened?" they demanded.
He replied, "The man they call Jesus made some mud and put it on my eyes. He told me to go to Siloam and wash. So I went and washed, and then I could see."
Where is this man?" they asked him.
"I don't know," he said. (John 9:7-12)
The man who had been healed only said what had happened to him. He wasn't afraid to answer a question with, "I don't know." But he was eager to speak up, no matter who was asking the questions.
They brought to the Pharisees the man who had been blind … (who) … also asked him how he had received his sight. "He put mud on my eyes," the man replied, "and I washed, and now I see."
Finally they turned again to the blind man, "What have you to say about him? It was your eyes he opened." The man replied, "He is a prophet." (John 9:13,17)

We read how the man went beyond describing his experiences to share his faith about who Jesus is. People won't always believe what we tell them but that should not surprise us – God does some pretty incredible, literally unbelievable things sometimes. We should keep on talking about Jesus anyway.
The Jews still did not believe that he had been blind and had received his sight until they sent for the man's parents. "Is this your son?" they asked. "Is this the one you say was born blind? How is it that now he can see?"
"We know he is our son," the parents answered, "and we know he was born blind. But how he can see now, or who opened his eyes, we don't know. Ask him. He is of age; he will speak for himself." (John 9:18-20)

Again the man only told people what he knew and wasn't afraid to say, "I don't know."
A second time they summoned the man who had been blind. "Give glory to God," they said. "We know this man is a sinner."
He replied, "Whether he is a sinner or not, I don't know. One thing I do know. I was blind but now I see!" (John 9:24-25)

We need to be patient and keep on answering people's questions.
Then they asked him, "What did he do to you? How did he open your eyes?"
He answered, "I have told you already and you did not listen. Why do you want to hear it again? … We know that God does not listen to sinners. He listens to the godly man who does his will. Nobody has ever heard of opening the eyes of a man born blind. If this man were not from God, he could do nothing." (John 9:26-27, 31-33)

The man who had been healed of blindness was now growing in his faith. Initially he only recognised that Jesus was a prophet. Now he says that Jesus must have come from God. It took another meeting with Jesus for the man to recognise that Jesus is Lord and to believe in Him. Yet the man was happy to talk about what had happened to him even before he fully put his trust in Jesus.

… When (Jesus) found him, he said, "Do you believe in the Son of Man?"
"Who is he, sir?" the man asked. "Tell me so that I may believe in him."
Jesus said, "You have now seen him; in fact, he is the one speaking with you."
Then the man said, "Lord, I believe," and he worshiped him. (John 9:35-38)

We won't have all the answers. That is fine. All we are called to do is tell people what we do know and be honest and brave about sharing what we believe. Remember how God healed the paralysed man at the Beautiful Gate of the Temple in Jerusalem. That man shared his testimony simply by walking and leaping and praising God and the people were filled with wonder and amazement.

Often when Christians use the word testimony, we are referring particularly to telling the story of how we became a Christian. Acts records two occasions in which Paul shared his testimony in that sense, first for a crowd in Jerusalem in Acts 22 and then before King Agrippa in Acts 26. We could learn much by looking at the different ways in which Paul tailored what he shared to suit his audience. But in both accounts there is a pattern which might be appropriate for many of us as we talk about what Jesus has done for us. Paul starts with what his life used to be like. Then he describes how he met Jesus and he finishes with the difference Jesus has made in his life. Before – how – after.

BEFORE: *"The Jews all know the way I have lived ever since I was a child, from the beginning of my life in my own country, and also in Jerusalem. They have known me for a long time and can testify, if they are willing, that according to the strictest sect of our religion, I lived as a Pharisee. … I too was convinced that I ought to do all that was possible to oppose the name of Jesus of Nazareth. … In my obsession against them, I even went to foreign cities to persecute them."* (Acts 26:4-5, 9, 11)

So Paul has explained just how far away from Jesus he had been. But one day that all changed – and he explains how.

HOW: *"On one of these journeys I was going to Damascus with the authority and commission of the chief priests. About noon, O king, as I was on the road, I saw a light from heaven, brighter than the sun, blazing around me and my companions. We all fell to the ground, and I heard a voice saying to me in Aramaic, 'Saul, Saul, why do you persecute me? It is hard for you to kick against the goads.'*
"Then I asked, 'Who are you, Lord?'
" 'I am Jesus, whom you are persecuting,' the Lord replied. 'Now get up and stand on your feet. I have appeared to you to appoint you as a servant and as a witness of what you have seen of me and what I will show you. … I am sending you to (the Gentiles) to open their eyes and turn them from darkness to light, and from the power of Satan to God, so that they may receive forgiveness of sins.'" (Acts 26:12-18)

Paul told the story of how he met with the Risen Jesus Christ on the Damascus Road, and he finished with the ways his life was different as a result. Before, how, then after.

AFTER: *"So then, King Agrippa, I was not disobedient to the vision from heaven. First to those in Damascus, then to those in Jerusalem and in all Judea, and to the Gentiles also, I preached that they should repent and turn to God and prove their repentance by their deeds."* (Acts 26:19-20)

We can notice how, to finish his testimony, Paul slips in a challenge and an invitation. Sometimes that may be appropriate for us to do – sometimes it won't. As Ecclesiastes 3:7 says, "There is a time to talk and a time to shut up." Sometimes we will only share how we became a Christian. Sometimes we will only talk about the difference Jesus is making to our lives today. In every case, it is really good to prepare ourselves to share those stories of "before, how and after" when the opportunity presents itself.

Paul also talked openly about other experiences he had of God's grace. He shared the suffering which came from his "thorn in the flesh."
Three times I pleaded with the Lord to take it away from me. But he said to me, "My grace is sufficient for you, for my power is made perfect in weakness." Therefore I will boast all the more gladly about my weaknesses, so that Christ's power may rest on me. That is why, for Christ's sake, I delight in weaknesses, in insults, in hardships, in persecutions, in difficulties. For when I am weak, then I am strong.
(2 Corinthians 12:8-10)

It is very important for Christians always to be honest in our testimonies; not to "gild the lily". We must be truthful about our questions and our doubts as well as about what we do know and believe and have experienced. If could very well be that the person we are speaking with is wrestling with questions and doubts. If we give the impression that we have got everything sorted and that we have all the answers that could leave them discouraged and depressed. If we are prepared to admit that we trust God even though we still have questions of our own, that will help other people to find faith too.

Paul was particularly honest and open with the Corinthians about the difficulties he himself had faced while he was preaching the gospel to them.
When I came to you, brothers, I did not come with eloquence or superior wisdom as I proclaimed to you the testimony about God. For I resolved to know nothing while I was with you except Jesus Christ and him crucified. I came to you in weakness and fear, and with much trembling. My message and my preaching were not with wise and persuasive words, but with a demonstration of the Spirit's power.
(1 Corinthians 2:1-4)

If the great apostle Paul felt *weakness and fear and much trembling,* we should not be surprised or worried if that is how we feel when we consider talking about Jesus. We do not rely on *wise and persuasive words.* The promise Jesus made about the help of the Holy Spirit was not just for the apostles and for Paul but for all of us.
"Whenever you are arrested and brought to trial, do not worry beforehand about what to say. Just say whatever is given you at the time, for it is not you speaking, but the Holy Spirit." (Mark 13:11)

On the basis of his own experiences, Paul was able to encourage Timothy with a similar promise.
For God did not give us a spirit of timidity, but a spirit of power, of love and of self-discipline. So do not be ashamed to testify about our Lord, or ashamed of me his prisoner. (2 Timothy 1:7-8)

All Christians have their own stories to tell about the difference Jesus has made and continues to make to their lives. It is very helpful to think through in advance what we might say when the door opens to talk about what God has done. Some people insist that we should not talk so much about ourselves and concentrate on talking about Jesus. But surely we need to be prepared to do either or both, depending on what our friend needs to hear. Sometimes it will be some part of the classic 'testimony' of how we came to faith: what our life was like before, how we met Jesus and how life has been different since. On other occasions it will be more appropriate to talk about how God continues to be involved in our daily lives, sharing experiences of healing and answers to prayer and specific ways Jesus has helped us. Our friends will trust our words because they know and trust the person who says them.

Since we really want to be confident and effective in talking about Jesus it can be helpful not only to prepare what we will say but also to practise sharing our stories with other Christians. We can do this one-to-one with a Christian friend, or in Home Groups or Cell Groups, or after the Sunday service in the time of fellowship over refreshments. North Springfield Baptist Church stayed together for Sunday bring-your-own lunches specifically to talk about Jesus together and to practise telling our stories to each other. There are also great blessings in writing our stories down and including them in the church's newsletter. At NSBC we went further and created a little self-published book called "The Difference Jesus Makes" which combined some testimonies of members in their own words with some gospel messages. As well as Christians giving this book to their friends, we offer a copy to everybody who visits any of our services, events and activities

The book *Finding Faith Today* discovered an under-reported fact. 27% of Christians surveyed said that the most important "supporting factor" in their journey to faith was "the Bible." [33] Among Baptist Christians, 22% considered that the Bible was the "main factor" in them becoming a Christian.[34] The Barna research similarly found that 27% of Christians felt that the Bible had a significant influence on them coming to faith.[35] We believe that God can speak powerfully through His Word the Bible not only to believers but also to not yet Christians (John 20:30-31; Hebrews 4:12). That's why it is a good thing for Christians to know by heart some key Bible verses and to be able to tell some Bible stories

---

33 John Finney *Finding Faith Today* BFBS 1992 37.

34 John Finney *Finding Faith Today* 61.

35 *Talking Jesus* booklet 23 at www.talkingjesus.org.

about Jesus when appropriate. Tim Chester helpfully suggests, "I always try to have a parable up my sleeve." It is also good for Christians and churches to take every opportunity to give gifts of New Testaments or Bibles in a modern translation and attractive presentation to folk who do not have them. Apart from Gideons International, nobody else is likely to do that. We can give or lend Christian books and church magazines to our friends and point them to Christian websites, blogs, and television and radio channels. Even an act as simple as sending explicitly Christian cards at Christmas can be a valuable witness. Any of these may also in time open the door for conversations as they did for Philip in Acts 8:30: *"Do you understand what you are reading?"*

Talking about Jesus is not about trotting out a twenty-minute presentation of the gospel. Christians simply need to answer our friends' questions about faith and spirituality and talk honestly and openly about the difference Jesus makes in our everyday lives. But it really helps if we can be prepared to give an answer and to take every opportunity. As Christians we are eager to have opportunities to talk about Jesus. We can make wise use of "faith flags" such as badges or jewellery with Christian symbols or posters displayed in windows to create opportunities for conversations. And sometimes the right thing to do is deliberately to initiate a conversation which gives our friend their opening to ask their questions. Here are a few questions which we can ask our friends which people find helpful in opening the door to talking about Jesus.

- What do you think is the point of life?
- How do you make sense of the world?
- On a bad day what makes you think that God doesn't exist?
- On a good day what makes you think that God might exist?
- How do you think everything all began?
- Who do you think Jesus was?
- Do you ever wonder what happens when we die?
- Have you ever prayed?

17 Ambassadors for Christ

As we seek to find ways to talk about Jesus more wisely and boldly, confidently and effectively, the apostle Paul's words to the Corinthians sum up both the gospel message and our role as Ambassadors for Christ.

Therefore, if anyone is in Christ, he is a new creation; the old has gone, the new has come! All this is from God, who reconciled us to himself through Christ and gave us the ministry of reconciliation: that God was reconciling the world to himself in Christ, not counting men's sins against them. And he has committed to us the message of reconciliation. We are therefore Christ's ambassadors, as though God were making his appeal through us. We implore you on Christ's behalf: Be reconciled to God. God made him who had no sin to be sin for us, so that in him we might become the righteousness of God. (2 Corinthians 5:17-21)

A brand new life

To begin with, Paul talks about the wonderful new life we enjoy as Christians. *Therefore, if anyone is in Christ, he is a new creation; the old has gone, the new has come.* Most translations say, *"He is a new creation"*, or *"he is a new person"*. Literally Paul says, "there is a new creation". The Message Translation puts it well. *"Anyone united with the Messiah gets a fresh start, is created new."* The meaning is even clearer in the Living Bible. *When someone becomes a Christian he becomes a brand new person inside. He is not the same any more. A new life has begun!*

Most religions are all about turning over a new leaf, working hard to become a better person, struggling to try to live up to God's standards. But becoming a Christian is not about turning over a new leaf. Becoming a Christian is about beginning a new life. God doesn't just call us to follow the example He has given us in Jesus Christ or just to live by Jesus's teachings. God actually makes it possible for us to share in Jesus's life! So as Christians we enjoy a brand new life. That newness of life is not just "less old", like changing to a newer car. Nor is it like so many washing powders are advertised, just some "new improved" version of the old. This is not the kind of superficial change you see in all those makeover programmes. God's work in our lives is not merely cosmetic surgery. It is a heart transplant. God gives us a brand new life – a dramatic transformation from the old, like the butterfly emerging from the caterpillar. But God does not want Christians to keep this amazing good news to ourselves.

Christians are Ambassadors for Christ

And he has committed to us the message of reconciliation. We are therefore Christ's ambassadors, as though God were making his appeal through us. We implore you on Christ's behalf: Be reconciled to God.

We are Christ's Ambassadors. We are His representatives. We are His Messengers. What an amazing privilege. And what an awesome responsibility, We could all name literally hundreds of famous people: monarchs; politicians; sports people and entertainers. Yet we probably could not name one single ambassador even though their importance as diplomats representing our nation around the world is enormous. Most of the time we haven't a clue who our ambassadors are despite their great influence. This is absolutely appropriate: the glorious task of an Ambassador is to draw attention to the one they are representing, not to themselves.

Ambassadors do not have any choice about whether they deliver their Sovereign's messages or not. That is their job: that is their responsibility. They may be scared of the reaction their message may provoke. But ambassadors don't have the option of staying silent. Their whole task is to represent their leader and speak on their behalf. And God appoints Christians to be Ambassadors for Christ. We may be scared of talking about Jesus and delivering the life-saving message of salvation. But we don't have a choice. Even the apostle Paul was scared of talking about Jesus, understandably because among many other sufferings Paul ended up in prison for preaching the gospel on many occasions! But he was conscious of his responsibility as an Ambassador for Christ and it is no coincidence that he used that very word when he was asking the church at Ephesus to pray for him.
'Pray also for me, that whenever I open my mouth, words may be given me so that I will fearlessly make known the mystery of the gospel, for which I am an ambassador in chains. Pray that I may declare it fearlessly, as I should." (Ephesians 6:19-20)

If we find ourselves anxious or afraid of fulfilling our responsibilities as Ambassadors for Christ, the one thing we should bear in mind is the source of an ambassador's authority. They never speak on their own authority. They always speak on the authority of the ruler who they represent. In the first century a Roman Ambassador was no less than the personal representative of the Roman Emperor himself. Similarly, Christians do not talk about Jesus on our own authority. We don't share the gospel on our own authority. We do so because Almighty God commands us to. He has entrusted to us the message of reconciliation.
… as though God were making his appeal through us. We implore you on Christ's behalf: Be reconciled to God. Here we are, then, speaking for Christ, as though God himself were making his appeal through us.

We are speaking for Christ, on His behalf. The message is not our message but God's message. We are not delivering the Good News on our authority but on the authority of the One we represent, even Almighty God. We speak because Jesus has authorised us and sent us to speak for him.
Jesus drew near and said to them, "I have been given all authority in heaven and on earth. Go, then, to all peoples everywhere and make them my disciples: baptize them in the name of the Father, the Son, and the Holy Spirit, and teach them to obey everything I have commanded you. And I will be with you always, to the end of the age." (Matthew 28:18-20)

When we share the gospel and talk about Jesus and seek to help others to become His disciples, we are doing so in obedience to the command of Jesus Himself; Jesus who God has declared to be the highest authority in heaven and on earth. Jesus Christ is King of Kings and Lord of Lords. And Jesus has appointed us to be his Ambassadors. We are his representatives, his messengers. We are simply delivering his wonderful Good News.

Jesus's Great Commission in Matthew 28 is not our only motive, nor even the most important motive for talking about Jesus. Earlier in that passage Paul says, "Christ's love compels us."
For Christ's love compels us, because we are convinced that one died for all, and therefore all died. And he died for all, that those who live should no longer live for themselves but for him who died for them and was raised again.
(2 Corinthians 5:14-15)

Paul wrote about the love of Christ. He is not talking about the love we have for Christ, although that should certainly be another motive for talking about Jesus. Rather, Paul is talking about Christ's love for us. Jesus loved us so much that He died for us. So we should live new lives, not doing whatever we want but doing what Jesus wants. Jesus died for our sins and was raised from the dead to give us this new life. When we realize just how much Jesus loves us, we will be so grateful we will want to tell other people about Jesus so they can come to experience this new life for themselves. Christ's love for us will indeed compel us to reach out with His love to our friends and neighbours and colleagues and even to strangers. God loves them too – and we will want them to know that!

Probably the greatest evangelical thinker of the 20th Century, Karl Barth wrote this about the church and about Christians being Ambassadors for Christ.

> "The church exists to preach the gospel. The life of the one holy Universal Church is determined by the fact that it is the fulfilment of the service as ambassador enjoined upon it."
>
> "Where the life of the Church is exhausted in self-serving, it smacks of death; the decisive thing has been forgotten, that this whole life is lived only in the exercise of what we called the Church's service as ambassador, in proclamation."
>
> "The 'Christ-believing group' … is sent out: 'Go and preach the gospel!' … In it all the one thing must prevail: 'Proclaim the gospel to every creature!' The Church runs like a herald to deliver the message. It is not a snail that carries its little house on its back and is so well off in it that only now and then it sticks out its feelers and then thinks that the 'claim of publicity' has been satisfied. No, the Church lives by its commission as herald."[36]

God has appointed us to be Ambassadors for Jesus. To drive home his point, Paul then explains the heart of God's masterplan of salvation.

The great exchange – our sins for God's righteousness

God made him who had no sin to be sin for us, so that in him we might become the righteousness of God. (2 Corinthians 5:21)

---

[36] K Barth *Dogmatics in Outline* 147.

This one verse explains perfectly the wonderful salvation Jesus obtained for us by His death on the cross. The Good News Bible translates the verse like this.
Christ was without sin, but for our sake God made him share our sin in order that in union with him we might share the righteousness of God.

God took the initiative in bringing us back to Himself. There was nothing we could do to make a way for us to know God. So God gave His one and only Son for us. And Jesus took all of our sin on Himself by dying on the cross. Jesus took the physical place which the notorious revolutionary Barabbas should have occupied on that middle cross between the two thieves. But far more importantly, Jesus took our place spiritually taking upon Himself the wrath of God. Jesus shared our sin. In fact, Paul says something even more amazing. Literally Paul says that the holy and sinless Son of God was made to be sin for us, on our behalf. Christ became sin. There on the cross, all the sin of humanity was separating the Father from the Son, splitting up the eternal Holy Trinity for our sakes, for our salvation, so that we might share and even become the righteousness of God. The Living Bible expresses this verse beautifully.
"For God took the sinless Christ and poured into him our sins. Then, in exchange, he poured God's goodness into us."

The second century Bishop Irenaeus explained the way of salvation like this. "Christ became what we are in order that we might become what he is." God became a human being so that we could become God's children. In the incarnation Christ shared in our humanity so that we could share in His divinity. On the cross Christ became sin so that we could become righteous. An old hymn puts it like this.
"Bearing shame and scoffing rude. In my place condemned He stood. Sealed my pardon with His blood. Hallelujah! What a Saviour!"

Martin Luther explained the gospel this way. "Lord Jesus, You are my righteousness but I am your sin. You took on You what was mine; You set on me what was Yours. You became what you were not that I might become what I was not." Graham Kendrick's hymn, "Father of the fatherless", uses another glorious image: "Exchanging for my wretchedness your radiant robes of righteousness"

This is the Good News. This is what Jesus has accomplished for us. These are the blessings His death on the Cross have bought for us. And this is the wonderful gospel we have to proclaim; the message which reconciles people to God. This is the Good News which changes people from God's enemies into God's friends and gives them a brand new life. This is the great exchange – our sin for God's righteousness. So God calls every Christian to live as an ambassador for Christ as we take this good news to a lost world.
We plead on Christ's behalf: let God change you from enemies into his friends! Christ was without sin, but for our sake God made him share our sin in order that in union with him we might share the righteousness of God.

Christians are all called to be Ambassadors for Christ. All of us wish we could do a better job representing Jesus to the people who do not know him. I have a recurring nightmare. It is that on my way to the Gates of Heaven I will have to walk up a path past all sorts of friends and neighbours I haven't seen for years. Past work colleagues and even members of my family who are shut outside never to enter. The nightmare is that I will hear each one of them saying to me, "You never told me." I knew the way to heaven, by God's grace I had found the way to eternal life, but they say to me, "You never told me. I never knew."

Christians are Ambassadors for Christ. We really need to make the best of every opportunity to talk about Jesus.

Afterword – Taking Every Opportunity

In the summer of 2015 North Springfield Baptist Church generously gave me a period of sabbatical leave to consider a simple question: "How can we help Contacts become Inquirers?" For many years, churches have seen the importance of working hard to serve and build relationships with their community. Churches run all kinds of activities and events, from Toddler Groups to Fun Days, from Holiday Clubs to cafés, from Food Banks to Community Choirs. But Contacts from these "Crossing Places" are rarely immediately ready to start attending church services or to sign up for popular Inquirers' Courses such as Alpha or Christianity Explored. What "stepping stones to faith" can we offer to bridge this gap? While visiting more than 20 churches and reading the books listed in the Bibliography I came to the conclusion that there is one obvious common feature in so many different approaches to this issue. The most important thing we can be doing is simply to be talking about Jesus. To initiate and develop conversations which explore spirituality and share faith. The Bible urges Christians always to be on the lookout for opportunities to talk about Jesus.

Be wise in the way you act toward outsiders; make the most of every opportunity. Let your conversation be always full of grace, seasoned with salt, so that you may know how to answer everyone. (Colossians 4:5-6)

Be very careful, then, how you live—not as unwise but as wise, making the most of every opportunity, because the days are evil. (Ephesians 5:15-16 NIV)

To help us all to make the most of every opportunity, churches and ministers need to equip Christians to be able to talk about Jesus wisely and confidently, boldly and effectively: to be able to initiate and develop conversations exploring and sharing faith and spirituality. It was evangelist D.L.Moody's guiding principle that "it is better to set ten men to work than to do the work of ten men". It is notable that not only pastor-teachers but also evangelists are given *"to prepare God's people for works of service"* (Ephesians 4:11-12) so that all Christians can share in the work of mission, witness, outreach and evangelism.

The resulting programme of sermons and study sessions was delivered in the autumn of 2015 and is now presented in this book. The Outline of that programme is available online, together with a collection of resources for Christians and churches entitled "42 Great Outreach Ideas." All this material can be found at www.takingeveryopportunity.org

Paul encouraged Timothy,
Preach the Word; be prepared in season and out of season. (2 Timothy 4:2 NIV).
Be prepared, whether the time is favorable or not. (New Living Translation)

Bill Hybels of Willow Creek holds out an exciting vision of what could happen as more Christians are empowered to talk about Jesus. "When ordinary Christians throughout the fabric of the church get trained and active in spreading their faith – you'd better watch out! A whole new era of lifechange is going to explode!"[37]

I was all prepared for one Sunday to preach a sermon on taking risks for the sake of the gospel. On the Saturday night I had a dream which I believe was prophetic. In the dream I was looking at the wall of our church and there I saw a painting. The painting showed fields next to a river on a bright sunny day. On the riverbank a large group of people were having a lovely time enjoying a picnic together as rowing boats went past along the river.

Then in my dream, next to that painting on the wall I saw another painting. It showed a scene further along the same river. Just round a bend, just out of view of the people having their picnic, there was a Niagara Falls sized waterfall. All the people in all the boats passing by were plunging to their deaths over the waterfall.

And all the time the people on the riverbank just went on enjoying their picnic. Nobody was throwing out lifelines to the boats passing by. Nobody was shouting out warnings to the boats. Nobody had even put up a sign saying, "Danger, waterfall ahead." They just went on with their picnic. Those were the two paintings I saw in my dream. The picnic and the waterfall.

---

[37] Bill Hybels *Becoming a Contagious Christian* Zondervan 1994 266-267.

The gospel of Jesus Christ *is the power of God for the salvation of everyone who believes.* (Romans 1:16) It is the message of Good News which is the difference between death and life for this lost world. Christians dare not be silent. We need to make the most of every opportunity to talk about Jesus. We need to be prepared to give an answer.

Bibliography

William Abraham *The Logic of Evangelism* Hodder 1989

Ben Alexander *Out of Darkness* College Press Pub Co 1985

Karl Barth *Dogmatics in Outline* Harper and Rowe 1959

Paul Beasley-Murray and Alan Wilkinson *Turning the Tide* Bible Society 1981

Mike Booker and Mark Ireland *Evangelism Which Way Now* Church House 2003

Walter Brueggemann *Biblical Perspectives on Evangelism* Abingdon Press 1993

Mark Cartledge *Testimony Its importance, place and potential* Grove Renewal 9 2002

Tim Chester *Mission Matters* IVP 2015

Stephen Cottrell *From the Abundance of the Heart* DLT 2006

Stephen Croft (editor) *Evangelism in a Spiritual Age* Church House Publishing 2005

Chris Duffet and Simon Goddard *Big Hearted* Gilead Books 2012

Evangelical Alliance, Church of England and Hope Together *Talking Jesus* at www.talkingjesus.org

John Finney *Finding Faith Today* BFBS 1992

Richard Foster *Prayer: Finding the heart's true home* HarperOne 1992, 2002

Mark Galli *"Speak* the Gospel : Use deeds when necessary." *Christianity Today* May 21, 2009

Jane Gibbs *Faith in Suburbia* Grove Booklets P95, 2003

Pete Gilbert *Kiss and Tell Evangelism as a Lifestyle* CWR 2003

Michael Gorman *Becoming the Gospel Paul, Participation and Mission* Eerdmans, Grand Rapids 2015

Michael Green *Evangelism now and then* IVP 1979

Michael Green *Evangelism Through the Local Church* Hodder 1990

Michael Green *You must be joking* Hodder 1976

Os Guinness *The Gravedigger File* Hodder 1983

Steve Hollinghurst, *Mission shaped Evangelism* Canterbury Press 2010

Hope the Heartbeat of Mission Hope08 Ltd 2013

George Hunter *Church for the Unchurched* Abingdon Press 1996

Bill Hybels *Becoming a Contagious Christian* Zondervan 1994

Andrew Kirk *Mission Under Scrutiny* DLT 2006

Steve Legg *The A-Z of Evangelism* Hodder 2002

Rebecca Manley Pippert *Out of the Saltshaker* IVP 1979

Mission-shaped Church Church House Publishing 2004

Stuart Murray *Post-Christendom* Paternoster 2004

Lesslie Newbigin *Foolishness to the Greeks* Eerdmans 1986

Pope Paul VI *Evangelii Nuntiandi* (encyclical on evangelization) 1974

Janice Price *Telling our faith story* Grove Evangelism 85, 1999 revised 2009

Chris Radley *Message on a Shoestring* MARC Europe 1986

Share Jesus International *Sharing Jesus* 2014 at www.sharejesusinternational.com

Lawrence Singlehurst *The Gospel Message Today* Grove Evangelism 100

Laurence Singlehurst *Sowing, Reaping, Keeping: People-sensitive Evangelism* IVP 2006

Nick Spencer *Beyond the Fringe Researching a Spiritual Age* Cliff College Publishing/LICC 2005

Emily Stimpson Blog at http://www.catholicvote.org/pope-francis-and-st-francis-preach-the-gospel-always-and-for-the-love-of-god-use-words/

Tim Sumpter *Evangelistening* Grove Evangelism 96 2011

Talking Jesus: Perceptions of Jesus, Christians and Evangelism in England at www.talkingjesus.org

Elmer Thiessen *The Ethics of Evangelism* Peternoster 2011

David Watson *I believe in Evangelism* Hodder 1976 Omnibus edition 1984

Also by Peter Thomas

Making Disciples One-To-One: Courses for Christian Growth. 2008

Peter posts all his Sermons and Studies online at **www.pbthomas.com/blog**.

He also reflects on aspects of theology, ministry and mission at **www.pbthomas.com/thoughts**.

Themes from this book are developed at **www.takingeveryopportunity.org**.

There are also a number of Peter's other writings on his website **www.pbthomas.com**.

Rev Peter Thomas has been a Baptist Minister for 30 years. After studying Natural Sciences and training as a teacher at Trinity Hall Cambridge he taught chemistry and computer studies for five years at Watford Grammar School. He then studied Theology at London Bible College (now London School of Theology) and was ordained in 1986.

Peter became Associate Minister of Tunbridge Wells Baptist Church where he also served for two years as President of Tunbridge Wells Council of Christian Churches. He moved to Borehamwood Baptist Church in 1991 and led them to plant Elstree Free Church. While there he received the MA in Biblical Interpretation from LBC. In 1999 Peter became Minister of Brentwood Baptist Church where he also served six years as Moderator and then three years as Secretary of Churches Together in Brentwood.

Since 2010 Peter has been Minister of North Springfield Baptist Church near Chelmsford in Essex. He currently serves on the Council of the Eastern Baptist Association leading the Task Group for Mission Resourcing and also as Treasurer of The College of Baptist Ministers.

Peter will very happy to discuss any of the topics covered in this book. Email **peter@pbthomas.com.**

MAKING DISCIPLES ONE-TO-ONE

Courses for Christian Growth – by Peter Thomas

Jesus Calls Us to be His Disciples

Twelve Great Reasons for Meeting One-to-One

Spiritual Friendships
Ideas to help established Christians begin meeting One-to-One.

One-to-One for New Christians
An eight session course on the basics of Christian discipleship for a person new to the Christian faith meeting with a Guide.

Fan the Flame
A course in discipleship for mature Christians: 25 challenging studies on five vital themes below each with a simple introduction, Bible passages and questions to consider – enhanced by regular meetings with a Guide.

Knowing God better
Loving God and enjoying your relationship with God; Devotional Bible reading and understanding the Bible; Worship; Your devotional prayer life; Intercessory prayer.

Becoming like Jesus
Repentance and Holiness; Christian Victory and Overcoming Temptation; The Renewed Mind; The Fruit of the Spirit and Mastering your Emotions; Total surrender to the Lordship of Christ.

Living in Christ's body
Forgiving yourself; Forgiving other people; Loving our Brothers and Sisters; Fellowship and Community; Being an Apprentice.

Becoming a servant
The Cross as our example of sacrifice; Serving in the church and in the world; Being a faithful Steward; Loving your neighbour; Our Witness to the World.

Be filled with the Spirit
Sharing Christ's resurrection life – the empowering Spirit; The gifts of the Holy Spirit – Serving in God's strength; Signs and wonders – the surprising Spirit; The Passion for God; Experiencing the Holy Spirit; Discipling others – how you being a Guide can help other Disciples.

SD - #0018 - 070726 - C0 - 234/156/8 - PB - 9781784563790 - Gloss Lamination